RESTING
IN HIS
SHADOW

DEVOTIONS
TO CLOSE THE DAY

BY CRISWELL FREEMAN

SMITH
FREEMAN
Publishing

About Criswell Freeman

Criswell Freeman is a Doctor of Clinical Psychology who, over the last 25 years, has authored numerous Christian, inspirational, and self-help titles. With over 20 million books in print, he usually avoids publicity and prefers to work quietly—and often anonymously—from his home in Nashville, Tennessee.

A Message to Readers

The English dramatist Thomas Dekker was correct when he observed, "Sleep is the golden chain that ties our health and our bodies together." A good night's sleep is, indeed, good for one's physical, spiritual, and emotional health. Yet we live in a media-saturated world that encourages us to spend more time glued to our screens and less time preparing for sleep.

Too much late-night screen time, combined with too little sleep, is a prescription for mental and physical exhaustion. And to make matters worse, we live in a stressed-out world brimming with an assortment of potential problems that can cause us to worry or to panic or both. So it's no wonder that so many of us are sleep deprived and anxious.

The Bible promises that we can "rest in the shadow of the Almighty" (Psalm 91:1 NIV) if we choose to do so. The ideas in this book are intended to help you rest in the Lord's shadow by encouraging you to focus, not on the world's problems, but upon God's solutions.

This text contains one hundred devotional readings that can provide comfort, assurance, and insight at the end of the day. If you're already in the habit of reading your Bible at night, the ideas on these pages will enrich that experience. But if you haven't formed the habit of consulting God's Word every night, you'll soon discover that when you talk to the Lord at the end of each day, He'll reward you with a renewed sense of perspective and peace. So for the next one hundred nights, try this experiment: read a chapter each evening and internalize the ideas that you find here. When you do, you'll discover the comfort, the power, and the peace that only the Lord can give. And as an added bonus, you'll sleep better.

Praying at the End of the Day

*Rejoice always, pray without ceasing, in everything give thanks;
for this is the will of God in Christ Jesus for you.*

1 THESSALONIANS 5:16–18 NKJV

It's the end of the day, and you're preparing for what you hope will be a good night's sleep. Before you turn out the lights, you probably have established some sort of routine that includes things like brushing your teeth, checking your messages, or making sure that the doors are locked. Depending on your circumstances, your pre-bedtime routine may be lengthy or it may be brief, but there's at least one item that should always be on your end-of-the-day checklist; prayer.

On his second missionary journey, Paul started a small church in Thessalonica. A short time later, he penned a letter that was intended to encourage the new believers at that church. Today, almost two thousand years later, 1 Thessalonians remains a powerful, practical guide for Christian living.

In his letter, Paul advised members of the new church to "pray without ceasing." His advice still applies. When we weave the habit of prayer into the fabric of our days *and* our nights, we invite God to become a partner in every aspect of our lives. So tonight and every night, allow God to guide you and help you. Pray without ceasing, and then rest assured that the Lord is listening to every word you say *and* pray.

A Prayer to End Your Day

Dear Lord, as I come to the end of this day, I thank you for another day. Because I know that you are with me, Father, I can complete this day with a sense of security and peace. Thank you, Lord, for Your blessings, Your protection, and Your Son. Amen.

2

Rest in His Shadow

Whoever dwells in the shelter of the Most High
will rest in the shadow of the Almighty.

PSALM 91:1 NIV

The Bible makes an interesting promise. In Psalm 91, God's Word promises that tonight, and every night, you can rest in God's shadow. If you make up your mind to do so, you can dwell "in the shelter of the Most High" by asking Him for protection. And that's an incredible blessing because, whether you realize it or not, you need the Lord's protection *and* His guidance.

In a world saturated with misleading messages, God is the ultimate truth. In a world filled with distractions and frustrations, He is the ultimate armor. In a world where bad news circles the globe before good news has time to circle the block, God restores your confidence and gives you hope.

The quality of your spiritual life will be in direct proportion to the quality of your prayer life. So tonight, instead of turning things over in your mind, turn them over to God in prayer. Instead of taking tomorrow's problems to bed with you, ask God to free you from your worries. Instead of talking to yourself, talk to your Creator. The Lord is listening, and He wants to hear from you before you drift off to sleep.

Tonight, like every other night, your heavenly Father invites you rest in His shadow. If you're wise, you'll accept His invitation.

A Prayer to End Your Day

Heavenly Father, at the conclusion of this day, I come to You with a grateful heart. You have given me another day of life, and You have offered me the priceless gift of eternal life through Your Son. Because You are with me always, Lord, I can rest tonight, knowing that you are my Shepherd and that I am protected. Amen.

Trust God and Be Confident

The Lord is my light and my salvation–whom should I fear?
The Lord is the stronghold of my life–of whom should I be afraid?
PSALM 27:1 HCSB

As Christians, we have every reason live confidently. After all, we've read God's promises and we know that He's prepared a place for us in heaven. And with God on our side, what should we fear? The correct answer, of course, is, nothing. But sometimes, despite our faith and despite God's promises, we find ourselves gripped by earthly apprehensions.

When we focus on our doubts and fears, we can concoct a lengthy list of reasons to lie awake at night and fret about the uncertainties of the coming day. A better strategy, of course, is to focus, not upon our fears, but instead upon our Creator.

Are you a confident Christian? You should be. God's promises never fail, and His love is everlasting. So the next time you need a boost of confidence, slow down and have a little chat with your Father. Count your blessings, not your troubles. Focus on possibilities, not problems. And remember that with God on your side, you have absolutely nothing to fear.

Faith in God is the greatest power, but great, too, is faith in oneself.
MARY MCLEOD BETHUNE

A Prayer to End Your Day

Heavenly Father, keep me mindful that I am a unique person, created by You, loved by You, and protected by You. When I put my confidence in You, Lord, I am secure. Tonight, Father, I will offer a prayer of thanksgiving, and I will place my trust in You. Amen.

4

Christ's Abundance

I have come that they may have life,
and that they may have it more abundantly.
JOHN 10:10 NKJV

The familiar words of John 10:10 convey this promise: Jesus came to this earth so that you might have a life of abundance. But what, precisely, did Christ mean when He talked of the abundant life? Was He promising to provide His followers with an abundance of earthly riches? Hardly. The Prince of Peace came to this world, not to give it prosperity, but to give it salvation. Thankfully, Christ's abundance is both spiritual and eternal; it never falters—even if we do—and it never dies. Your task, as a follower of the One from Galilee, is to accept Christ's abundance and to claim His gifts.

The fullness of life in Christ can—and should—be yours, but no one can claim those riches on your behalf; you must claim them for yourself. When you do, you will receive the love and the abundance that He has promised. So tonight, make this promise to yourself: promise that you will forge a genuine relationship with Jesus. And then claim to the joy, the peace, and the spiritual abundance that the Shepherd offers His sheep.

God loves you and wants you to experience
peace and life–abundant and eternal.
BILLY GRAHAM

A Prayer to End Your Day

Dear Lord, You have offered me the gift of abundance through Your Son. Tonight, I thank You, Father, for the abundant life that is mine through Christ Jesus. With a grateful heart, I will accept Christ's gifts and use them always to glorify You. Amen.

5

Banishing Anxiety
before the End of the Day

*Be anxious for nothing, but in everything by prayer and supplication,
with thanksgiving, let your requests be made known to God.*

PHILIPPIANS 4:6 NKJV

We live in a fast-paced, stress-inducing, anxiety-filled world that oftentimes seems to shift beneath our feet. Sometimes, trusting God is difficult, especially when we become caught up in the incessant demands and the constant distractions that are woven into the fabric of twenty-first-century life.

When it's time for sleep, you may still feel stressed by the demands of your day or, more likely, by the negative news you've heard along the way. If so, your nighttime challenge is simply this: you must return your thoughts to God's love, God's protection, and God's promises. Then, as you say a prayer at the end of the day, you should turn all of your concerns over to your heavenly Father.

The same God who created the universe will comfort you if you ask Him. Ask Him. Thank Him for His blessings and remind yourself that He is your shepherd. When you do, you can turn off the lights, knowing that earthly problems are temporary, but God's love lasts forever.

A Prayer to End Your Day

Lord, sometimes this world is a difficult place, and, as a frail human being, I become anxious. When I am worried, restore my faith. When I am anxious, turn my thoughts to You. When I grieve, touch my heart with Your enduring love. And keep me mindful, Lord, that nothing, absolutely nothing, is impossible for You. Thank You, Father, for loving me and protecting me, now and forever. Amen.

He's Right Here, Right Now

The LORD is with you when you are with Him.
If you seek Him, He will be found by you.
2 CHRONICLES 15:2 HCSB

Since God is everywhere, we are free to sense His presence whenever we take the time to quiet our souls and turn our prayers to Him. But sometimes, amid the incessant demands of everyday life, we turn our thoughts far from God. when we do, we suffer.

Do you set aside quiet moments at the end of each day to offer praise to your Creator? As a person who has received the gift of God's grace, you most certainly should. Silence is a gift that you give to yourself and to the Lord. During these moments of stillness, you may sense the infinite love and power of your Creator—and He, in turn, may speak directly to your heart.

The familiar words of Psalm 46:10 remind us to "Be still, and know that I am God" (NIV). When we do so, we encounter the awesome presence of our loving heavenly Father, and we are comforted in the knowledge that God is not just near. He is here.

The knowledge that we are never alone calms the troubled sea
of our lives and speaks peace to our souls.
A. W. TOZER

A Prayer to End Your Day

Heavenly Father, help me feel Your presence in every situation and every circumstance. You are with me, Lord, in times of celebration and in times of sorrow. You are with me when I am strong and when I am weak. Tonight, Father, as I prepare for sleep, I can be at peace, knowing that You are with me always. Amen.

He Renews Your Spirit

You are being renewed in the spirit of your minds;
you put on the new self, the one created according to
God's likeness in righteousness and purity of the truth.

EPHESIANS 4:23–24 HCSB

For busy citizens of the twenty-first century, it's easy to become overcommitted, overworked, and overstressed. If we choose, we can be connected 24-7, sparing just enough time to a get few hours' sleep each night. A better strategy is to carve out time in the evening to spend a few moments with God.

God will comfort you if you let Him. But He won't force you to slow down; He won't insist that you get enough sleep at night; and He won't demand that you spend a few quiet moments with Him before you turn off the lights. He leaves those choices up to you.

If you're feeling chronically tired or discouraged, it's time to rearrange your schedule, turn off your screens, and spend quiet time with your Creator. He knows what you need, and He wants you to experience His peace and His love. He's ready, willing, and perfectly able to renew your spirit if you ask Him. In fact, He's ready to hear your prayers right now. Please don't make Him wait.

No matter how badly we have failed, we can always get up
and begin again. Our God is the God of new beginnings.

WARREN WIERSBE

A Prayer to End Your Day

Dear Lord, when I am tired or worried, You can renew my spirit and restore my strength. When I need to change, Lord, change me. And then, with love in my heart and praise on my lips, let me live courageously and follow faithfully in the footsteps of Your Son. Amen.

God's Roadmap for Life

*All Scripture is inspired by God and is profitable for teaching,
for rebuking, for correcting, for training in righteousness, so that
the man of God may be complete, equipped for every good work.*

2 TIMOTHY 3:16–17 HCSB

God's Word is unlike any other book. The Bible is a roadmap for life here on earth and for life eternal. As Christians, we are called upon to study God's Holy Word, to follow its commandments, and to share its Good News with the world. To do otherwise is to deprive ourselves of a priceless gift from the Creator.

The Bible is a book of promises. And when God makes a promise, He keeps it. No exceptions. Bible promises are not hypotheticals; they're certainties. Those promises apply to every generation, including yours, and they apply to every human being, including you.

Jonathan Edwards advised, "Be assiduous in reading the Holy Scriptures. This is the fountain whence all knowledge in divinity must be derived. Therefore let not this treasure lie by you neglected." God's Holy Word is, indeed, a priceless, one-of-a-kind treasure, and a passing acquaintance with the Good Book is insufficient for Christians who seek to obey God's Word and to understand His will. After all, neither man nor woman lives by bread alone . . .

A Prayer to End Your Day

Heavenly Father, Your Word is a light unto the world; I will study it and trust it, and share it. In all that I do, help me be a worthy witness for You as I share the Good News of Your perfect Son and Your perfect Word. Amen.

Keep Dreaming

With God's power working in us, God can do much,
much more than anything we can ask or imagine.
EPHESIANS 3:20 NCV

Are you excited about tomorrow's opportunities and possibilities? Do you confidently expect God to lead you to a place of abundance, peace, and joy? And when your days on earth are over, do you expect to receive the priceless gift of eternal life? If you trust God's promises, and if you have welcomed God's Son into your heart, then you should believe that your future is intensely and eternally bright.

God has big plans for you, and He has equipped you with everything you need to make His plans come true. When the dream in your heart is one that God has placed there, miracles happen. Your challenge, of course, is to make certain that God's plans and your dreams coincide.

So keep believing in yourself, keep talking to your Creator, and keep working. And don't be afraid to dream big. After all, with God as your partner, there's no limit to the things that the two of you, working together, can accomplish.

Allow your dreams a place in your prayers and plans. God-given
dreams can help you move into the future He is preparing for you.
BARBARA JOHNSON

A Prayer to End Your Day

Dear Lord, as I come to the end of this day, I can have hope because You are with me. You give me the courage to face the future with certainty; I ask that You give me the wisdom to follow closely in the footsteps of Your Son, now and forever. Amen.

10

Surrender and Trust

A man's heart plans his way, but the LORD determines his steps.
PROVERBS 16:9 HCSB

Sometimes, we must accept life on its terms, not our own. Life has a way of unfolding, not as we will, but as it will. And sometimes, there is precious little we can do to change things.

When events transpire that are beyond our control, we have a choice: we can either learn the art of acceptance, or we can make ourselves miserable as we struggle to change the unchangeable.

When we encounter a problem that we simply cannot fix, or a situation we cannot change, we should surrender it to the Lord and trust His infinite wisdom. Then, having accepted reality, we can prayerfully and faithfully tackle the things that we can change.

Tonight as you survey the landscape of your life, can you summon the courage and the wisdom to accept the things that are simply too big for you to repair on your own? Hopefully so. When you learn the art of acceptance, you'll find comfort in the knowledge that your Creator is good, that His love endures forever, and that He understands His plans perfectly, even when you do not.

A Prayer to End Your Day

Dear Lord, tonight I ask that You let me live in the present, not the past. Let me focus on my blessings, not my sorrows. Give me the wisdom to be thankful for the gifts that I do have, and not to be bitter about the things that I don't have. Let me accept what was; let me give thanks for what is; and let me have faith in what most surely will be: the promise of eternal life with You. Amen.

Ask Him

*Ask, and it will be given to you; seek, and you will find; knock,
and it will be opened to you. For everyone who asks receives,
and he who seeks finds, and to him who knocks it will be opened.*

MATTHEW 7:7–8 NKJV

Genuine, heartfelt prayer produces powerful changes in us and in our world. When we lift our hearts to God, we open ourselves to a never-ending source of divine wisdom and infinite love. Jesus made it clear to His disciples: they should ask the Lord to meet their needs. So should we.

Do you have questions about your future that you simply can't answer? Do you have needs that you simply can't meet by yourself? Do you sincerely seek to know God's unfolding plan for your life? If so, ask Him for direction, for protection, and for strength—and then keep asking Him until the answer becomes clear.

God is not just near; He is here, and He's perfectly capable of answering your prayers. But it's up to you to ask.

*We honor God by asking for great things when they are a part
of His promise. We dishonor Him and cheat ourselves when we ask
for molehills where He has promised mountains.*

VANCE HAVNER

A Prayer to End Your Day

Dear Lord, give me the wisdom to ask You for the things I need. In every situation, let me come to You in prayer. You know my hopes and, more importantly, You know my needs. So I will ask You, Father, for the things that I think I need, and then I will trust the answer that You give. Amen.

12

Trust Him When Times Are Tough

*Praise the God and Father of our Lord Jesus Christ, the Father
of mercies and the God of all comfort. He comforts us in all our
affliction, so that we may be able to comfort those who are in any
kind of affliction, through the comfort we ourselves receive from God.*

2 CORINTHIANS 1:3-4 HCSB

The Bible promises this: tough times are temporary but God's love is not—God's love lasts forever. So what does that mean to you? Just this: from time to time, everybody faces tough times, and so will you. And when tough times arrive, God will always stand ready to protect you and heal you.

Psalm 147 promises, "He heals the brokenhearted" (v. 3, NIV), but Psalm 147 doesn't say that He heals them instantly. Usually, it takes time (and maybe even a little help from you) for God to fix things. So if you're facing tough times, face them with God by your side. If you find yourself in any kind of trouble, pray about it and ask God for His help. And be patient. The Lord will work things out, just as He has promised, but He will do it in His own way and in His own time. He is a God of possibility, not negativity, so you can rest assured that He will guide you through your difficulties and beyond them. Then with a renewed spirit of optimism and hope, you can thank the Giver for gifts that are simply too numerous to count.

A Prayer to End Your Day

Dear heavenly Father, You are my strength and my protector. When I am troubled, You comfort me. When I am discouraged, You lift me up. When I am afraid, You deliver me. In times of adversity, I will trust Your plan and Your will for my life. Your love is infinite, Lord, as is Your wisdom. As I come to the end of this day, keep me mindful that You are firmly in control, and that Your love endures forever. Amen.

13

Making Peace with the Past

There is one thing I always do. Forgetting the past and straining toward what is ahead, I keep trying to reach the goal and get the prize for which God called me.

PHILIPPIANS 3:13–14 NCV

In the third chapter of Philippians, Paul instructs us to focus on the future, not the past. Yet for many of us, focusing on the future is difficult indeed. Why? Part of the problem has to do with forgiveness. When we find ourselves focusing too intently on the past, it's a sure sign that we need to focus, instead, on a more urgent need: the need to forgive. Until we thoroughly and completely forgive those who have hurt us, we inevitably remain stuck in the past, both spiritually *and* emotionally.

No amount of anger or bitterness can change what happened yesterday. Tears can't change the past; regrets can't change it; our worries won't change the past, and neither will our complaints. Simply put, the past is, and always will be, the past. Forever. So if you've endured difficult circumstances, learn from them, but don't live with them. Instead, build your future on a firm foundation of trust and forgiveness—trust in your heavenly Father, and forgiveness for all His children, including yourself.

A Prayer to End Your Day

Heavenly Father, free me from anger, resentment, and envy. When I am bitter, I cannot feel the peace that You intend for me to experience. So help me accept the past, treasure the present, and entrust the future to You. Amen.

14

From Darkness to Light

Though I sit in darkness, the LORD will be my light.
MICAH 7:8 HCSB

Have you ever faced a challenge that seemed too big to handle? Have you ever faced a problem that, despite your best efforts, simply could not be resolved? If so, you know how uncomfortable it is to feel helpless in the face of difficult circumstances. Thankfully, even when there's nowhere else to turn, you can always turn your thoughts and prayers to the Lord, knowing that He is always with you.

When we are weary, the Lord gives us strength. When we lose hope, God reminds us of His promises. When we grieve, our heavenly Father wipes away our tears.

God gives comfort and power to those who turn their hearts and prayers to Him. Count yourself among that number. When you do, you can live courageously and joyfully, knowing that "this too will pass"—but that God's love for you will never end.

The safest place in all the world is in the will of God, and the safest protection in all the world is the name of God.
WARREN WIERSBE

A Prayer to End Your Day

Lord, sometimes life is difficult. Sometimes, I am worried, weary, or heartbroken. But when I lift my eyes to You, Father, You strengthen me. When I am weak, You lift me up. Tonight, keep me mindful that I can always turn to You for strength, for hope, for guidance, and for peace. Amen.

15

The Power of Forgiveness

For if you forgive people their wrongdoing, your heavenly Father
will forgive you as well. But if you don't forgive people,
your Father will not forgive your wrongdoing.

MATTHEW 6:14–15 HCSB

The world holds few if any rewards for those who remain angrily focused upon the past. Still, the act of forgiveness is difficult for most of us. Being frail, fallible, imperfect human beings, we can be quick to anger, quick to blame, slow to forgive, and even slower to forget. Yet as Christians, we are commanded to forgive others, just as we, too, have been forgiven.

For those who seek to follow in Christ's footsteps, forgiveness isn't optional. Jesus didn't say, "Forgive people when you feel like it," or "Forgive others when it's easy." Instead, Jesus instructed His followers to forgive quickly, completely, and repeatedly:

> "Then Peter came to Him and said, 'Lord, how often shall my brother sin against me, and I forgive him? Up to seven times?' Jesus said to him, 'I do not say to you, up to seven times, but up to seventy times seven'" (Matthew 18:21–22 NKJV)

Christ's instructions to Peter also apply to each of us. We are commanded—not encouraged, not advised; we are commanded—to forgive and to keep forgiving, even when it's hard.

A Prayer to End Your Day

Dear Lord, let forgiveness rule my heart even when forgiveness is difficult. Let me be Your obedient servant, Lord, and let me be a person who forgives others just as You have forgiven me. Amen.

16

Be Cheerful and Be Grateful

Worry is a heavy load, but a kind word cheers you up.
PROVERBS 12:25 NCV

Cheerfulness is a gift that we give to others and to ourselves. And as believers who have been saved by a risen Christ, why shouldn't we be cheerful? The answer, of course, is that we have every reason to honor our Savior with joy in our hearts, smiles on our faces, and words of celebration on our lips.

Christ promises us lives of abundance and joy if we accept His love and His grace. Yet sometimes, even the most righteous among us are beset by fits of ill temper and frustration. During these moments, we may not feel like turning our thoughts and prayers to the Lord, but that's precisely what we should do. When we consider all the things that God has done for us, we simply can't stay grumpy for long.

So tonight, as you think about the direction of your life, make this promise to yourself and keep it: be a cheerful ambassador for Christ. Jesus deserves no less. His heavenly Father deserves no less, and neither, for that matter, do you.

*God is good, and heaven is forever. And if those
two facts don't cheer you up, nothing will.*
MARIE T. FREEMAN

A Prayer to End Your Day

Heavenly Father, You have given me so many reasons to celebrate life here on earth and eternal life in heaven. Tonight, I ask for the wisdom to be a cheerful Christian as I celebrate Your incomparable gifts and contemplate Your never-ending love. Amen.

17

Keep Counting Your Blessings

Therefore, with your minds ready for action, be serious and set your hope completely on the grace to be brought to you at the revelation of Jesus Christ.

1 PETER 1:13 HCSB

As you prepare yourself for a good night's sleep, take a few moments to count your blessings. Those blessings are, in fact, too numerous to count, but it never hurts to try.

Billy Graham had sound advice for believers of all ages. He said, "Think of the blessings we so easily take for granted: Life itself; preservation from danger; every bit of health we enjoy; every hour of liberty; the ability to see, to hear, to speak, to think, and to imagine all this comes from the hand of God." And he was right.

Because all of us have been so richly blessed, we should make thanksgiving a habit, a regular part of our daily routines. But sometimes, amid the stresses and obligations of everyday life, we may allow interruptions and distractions to interfere with the time we spend with God.

The Lord has blessed you in many ways. His gifts include your family, your friends, your talents, your opportunities, your possessions, and the priceless gift of eternal life. These blessings are priceless, and the Lord is responsible for every one of them. So it's never too soon—or too late—to offer Him thanks.

A Prayer to End Your Day

Tonight, dear Lord, I will continue to count my blessings, although I realize that Your incredible gifts are actually too numerous to count. You are the Giver of all things good, and You have richly blessed my life. Now I ask that You help me find ways to share my blessings with others. And may the glory be Yours forever. Amen.

18
Your Very Bright Future

"For I know the plans I have for you"–this is the Lord's declaration–
"plans for your welfare, not for disaster, to give you a future and a hope."
JEREMIAH 29:11 HCSB

If you've entrusted your heart to Christ, your eternal fate is secure and your future is eternally bright. No matter how troublesome your present circumstances may seem, you can live courageously because the Lord has promised that you are His now and forever.

Of course, the Bible doesn't guarantee that your life here on earth will be trouble free. While you're here, you'll probably experience your fair share of setbacks, disappointments, emergencies, and outright failures. But these are only temporary defeats.

Are you willing to place your future in the hands of a loving and all-knowing God? Do you trust in the ultimate goodness of His plan for you? Will you face tomorrow's challenges with hope and optimism? You should. After all, God created you for a very important purpose: His purpose. And you still have important work to do: His work. So tonight, as you give thanks for the day's blessings and look forward to tomorrow's opportunities, remember that God has a marvelous plan for you and your loved ones. It's a beautiful thought—and a wonderful way—to bring a happy ending to your day.

Knowing that your future is absolutely assured
can free you to live abundantly today.
SARAH YOUNG

A Prayer to End Your Day

Dear Lord, as I look to the future, I will place my trust in You. If I become discouraged, I will turn to You. If I am afraid, I will seek strength in You. You are my Father, and I will place my hope, my trust, and my faith in You. Amen.

When Mountains Need Moving

I assure you: If anyone says to this mountain, "Be lifted up and thrown into the sea," and does not doubt in his heart, but believes that what he says will happen, it will be done for him.

MARK 11:23 HCSB

The Bible makes it clear: faith is powerful. With it, we can move mountains. With it, we can endure any hardship. With it, we can rise above the challenges of everyday life and live victoriously, whatever our circumstances.

Is your faith strong enough to move the mountains in your own life? If so, you've already tapped in to a source of strength that never fails: God's strength. But if your spiritual batteries are in need of recharging, don't be discouraged. God's strength is always available to those who seek it.

The first element of a successful life is faith: faith in God, faith in His promises, and faith in His Son. When our faith in the Creator is strong, we can then have faith in ourselves, knowing that we are tools in the hands of a loving God who made mountains—and moves them—according to a perfect plan that only He can see.

I beg you to recognize the extreme simplicity of faith; it is nothing more nor less than just believing God when He says He either has done something for us, or will do it; and then trusting Him to do it. It is so simple that it is hard to explain.

HANNAH WHITALL SMITH

A Prayer to End Your Day

Lord, sometimes this world is a frightening place. When I am filled with uncertainty and doubt, give me faith. In life's dark moments, help me remember that You are always near and that You can overcome any challenge. Tonight, tomorrow, and forever, I will place my trust in You. Amen.

20

Contagious Christianity

Genuine, heartfelt Christianity can be highly contagious, and that fits in nicely with God's plans for humanity. When we've experienced the transforming power of God's love, He wants us to share our faith with family, with friends, and with the world.

Every believer, bears responsibility for sharing God's Good News. And it is important to remember that you share your testimony not only through your words, but also through your actions.

So don't be a quiet Christian, and don't keep your faith to yourself. Instead, talk about Jesus and, while you're at it, show the world what it really means to follow Him. So tomorrow morning, and every day after that, make it a point to talk about your faith and to demonstrate your faith. But not necessarily in that order.

A Prayer to End Your Day

Thank You, Lord, for Your Son. His love is boundless, infinite, and eternal. Tonight, I will pause and reflect upon Christ's love for me. And tomorrow, I will strive to share Your love *and* the Good News of Your Son with all those who cross my path. Amen.

21

Experiencing Joy

Oswald Chambers observed, "Joy is the great note all throughout the Bible." C. S. Lewis echoed that thought when he wrote, "Joy is the serious business of heaven." But even the most dedicated Christians can, on occasion, forget to recognize each day for what it is: a priceless gift from God.

Psalm 100 reminds us to celebrate the lives that God has given us: "Shout for joy to the LORD, all the earth. Worship the LORD with gladness; come before him with joyful songs."

(vv. 1–2 NIV). Yet sometimes, amid the inevitable complications and predicaments that are woven into the fabric of everyday life, we forget to rejoice. Instead of celebrating life, we complain about it. As Christians, we are called by our Creator to live joyfully and abundantly. To do otherwise is to squander His spiritual gifts.

Tonight, tomorrow, and every day after that, Christ offers you His peace, His abundance, and His joy. Accept it and share it with others, just as He has shared His joy with you.

A Prayer to End Your Day

Heavenly Father, make me a joyful Christian. I have every reason to celebrate life. Let me share the Good News of Jesus Christ, and let my life be a testimony to His love and to His grace. Amen.

22

Listening to God

Sometimes God speaks loudly and clearly. More often, He speaks in a quiet voice, and if you're wise, you will be listening carefully when He does. To do so, you must carve out quiet moments to study His Word and sense His guidance.

Can you quiet yourself long enough to listen to your conscience? Are you attuned to the subtle guidance of your intuition? Are you willing to pray sincerely and then to wait quietly for God's response? Hopefully so. Usually God refrains from sending His messages on stone tablets or city billboards. More often, He communicates in subtler ways. If you sincerely desire to hear His voice, you must listen carefully, and you must do so in the silent corners of your quiet, willing heart.

A Prayer to End Your Day

Lord, give me the wisdom to be a good listener. Help me listen carefully to my family, to my friends, and—most importantly—to You. Amen.

Fear Not

He will not fear bad news; his heart is confident,
trusting in the LORD. His heart is assured; he will not fear.

PSALM 112:7–8 HCSB

Life can be difficult and discouraging at times. During our darkest moments, God offers us strength and courage if we turn our hearts and our prayers to Him. But sometimes, because we are imperfect human beings who possess imperfect faith, we fall prey to fear and doubt. The answer to our fears, of course, is God.

Every person's life is a tapestry of events: some wonderful, some not so wonderful, and some downright disastrous. When we visit the mountaintops of life, praising God isn't hard—in fact, it's easy. In our moments of triumph, we can bow our heads and thank God for our victories. But when we fail to reach the mountaintops, when we endure the inevitable losses that are a part of every person's life, we find it much harder to give God the praise He deserves.

Wherever we find ourselves, whether on the mountaintops of life or in life's darkest valleys, we must still offer thanks to God, giving thanks in all circumstances. And we must trust Him on good days, and bad days, and all the days in between. So the next time you find your courage tested to the limit, remember that God is as near as your next breath. He is your shield and your strength; He is your protector and your deliverer. Call upon Him in your hour of need and then be comforted. Whatever your challenge, whatever your trouble, God can handle it . . . and He will!

A Prayer to End Your Day

Heavenly Father, fill me with Your Spirit and help me face my challenges with courage and determination. Keep me mindful, Lord, that You are with me always, and with You by my side, I have nothing to fear. Amen.

24

Let God Help You
Make Better Decisions

If you need wisdom, ask our generous God,
and he will give it to you. He will not rebuke you for asking.

JAMES 1:5 NLT

The world will often lead you astray, but God will not. So the key to making good decisions is prayer. The bigger the decision, the more you should pray about it.

From the instant you wake in the morning until the moment you nod off to sleep at night, you have the opportunity to make countless choices: choices about the things you do, choices about the words you speak, and choices about the thoughts you choose to think. Simply put, the quality of those choices determines, to a surprising extent, the quality of your life.

Are you willing to invest the time, the effort, and the prayers that are required to make wise decisions? Are you willing to take your concerns to the Lord and to avail yourself of the messages and mentors that He has placed along your path? If you answered yes to these questions, you'll make better decisions, decisions which, by the way, will lead directly and inexorably to a better life.

I don't doubt that the Holy Spirit guides your decisions from within when you make them with the intention of pleasing God. The error would be to think that He speaks only within, whereas in reality He speaks also through Scripture, the Church, Christian friends, books, etc.

C. S. LEWIS

A Prayer to End Your Day

Lord, help me to make decisions that are pleasing to You. Help me to be honest, patient, thoughtful, and obedient. And above all, help me follow the teachings of Jesus, not just tonight or tomorrow, but every day of my life. Amen.

Confident Christianity

You are my hope; O Lord GOD, You are my confidence.
PSALM 71:5 NASB

Even the most faithful Christians are overcome by occasional bouts of fear and doubt. You are no different. Every life—including yours—is a series of successes and failures, celebrations and disappointments, hopes and doubts, joys and sorrows. But even when you feel very distant from God, you must remember that God is never distant from you. When you sincerely seek His presence, He will touch your heart, calm your fears, and restore your confidence.

Doubts come in several shapes and sizes: doubts about God, doubts about the future, and doubts about your own abilities, for starters. And what, precisely, does God's Word say in response to these doubts? The Bible is clear: when you are beset by doubts, of whatever kind, you must draw closer to the Lord through worship and through prayer.

God is always with you, always willing to calm the storms of life. When you sincerely seek His presence—and when you genuinely seek to establish a deeper, more meaningful relationship with His Son—the Lord is prepared to touch your heart, to calm your fears, to answer your doubts, and to restore your confidence.

Bible hope is confidence in the future.
WARREN WIERSBE

A Prayer to End Your Day

Lord, when I place my confidence in the things of this earth, I will be disappointed. But when I put my confidence in You, I am secure. In every aspect of my life, Father, let me place my hope and my trust in Your infinite wisdom and Your boundless grace. Amen.

Dealing with Disappointments

Give your burdens to the LORD, and he will take care of you.
He will not permit the godly to slip and fall.

PSALM 55:22 NLT

From time to time, all of us face life-altering disappointments. Oftentimes these disappointments come unexpectedly, leaving us with more questions than answers. But even when we don't have all the answers—or, for that matter, even when we don't seem to have *any* of the answers—God does. Whatever our circumstances, whether we stand atop the highest mountain or wander through the darkest valley, God is ready to protect us, to comfort us, and to heal us. Our task is to let Him.

If you've endured a life-altering disappointment, you may have good reason to ask, "Where do you want me to go from here, Lord?" His answer may not come immediately, and it may not come in a way that you expect, but of this you can be certain: if you sincerely ask, God will answer (Matthew 7:7–8).

Your heavenly Father has a perfect plan and a chosen path for all of His children, including you. When tough times arrive, you should learn from your experiences and you should prayerfully seek God's guidance for the future. Then you should get busy with the work at hand—the difficult and rewarding work of overcoming your disappointments. When you do your part, you can be certain that God will do His part. In time, your loving heavenly Father will turn your stumbling blocks into stepping stones.

A Prayer to End Your Day

Heavenly Father, when I suffer the inevitable setbacks of life, remind me that You are in control. You are the Giver of all good things, Father, and You will bless me tonight, tomorrow, and forever. Amen.

Beyond Bitterness

All bitterness, anger and wrath, shouting and slander must be removed from you, along with all malice. And be kind and compassionate to one another, forgiving one another, just as God also forgave you in Christ.

EPHESIANS 4:31–32 HCSB

The world holds few if any rewards for those who remain angrily focused upon the past. Still, the act of forgiveness can be difficult. Being frail, fallible, imperfect human beings, most of us are quick to anger, quick to blame, slow to forgive, and even slower to forget. Yet as Christians, we are commanded to forgive others, just as we, too, have been forgiven.

Are you mired in the quicksand of bitterness or regret? If so, you are not only disobeying God's Word, you are also wasting your time. So if there exists even one person—alive or dead—against whom you hold bitter feelings, it's time to forgive. Or if you are embittered against yourself for some past mistake or shortcoming, it's finally time to forgive yourself and move on. Hatred, bitterness, and regret are not part of God's plan for your life. Forgiveness is.

A Prayer to End Your Day

Heavenly Father, tonight I ask that you free me from the emotional chains of anger and bitterness. When I am angry, I forfeit Your peace. When I am bitter, I stir up feelings that are harmful to my spirit. So I ask for the wisdom and the strength to turn away from bitterness so that I can claim the spiritual abundance that You offer to those who follow closely in the footsteps of Your Son. Amen.

28

Ending the Day
with a Positive Attitude

Finally brothers, whatever is true, whatever is honorable,
whatever is just, whatever is pure, whatever is lovely,
whatever is commendable–if there is any moral excellence
and if there is any praise–dwell on these things.

PHILIPPIANS 4:8 HCSB

How will you direct your thoughts tonight? As you prepare for a good night's sleep, will you consider the words of Philippians 4:8 by dwelling upon those things that are honorable, just, and commendable? Or will you allow your thoughts to be hijacked by the negativity that seems to dominate our troubled world? Your answer will help determine the quality of your sleep *and* the quality of your life.

Take a few moments to consider your attitudes and your emotions. Are you fearful, angry, bored, or worried? Are you so preoccupied with the concerns of everyday life that you fail to thank God for the promise of eternity? Are you confused, bitter, or pessimistic? If so, God wants to have a little talk with you.

Your heavenly Father intends that you experience joy and abundance. So tonight and every night, take a few moments to celebrate the life that God has given you by focusing your thoughts upon things that are worthy of praise. Count your blessings instead of your hardships. And thank the Giver of all things good for gifts that are simply too numerous to count.

A Prayer to End Your Day

Dear Lord, tonight I pray for an attitude that is Christ-like. Whatever my circumstances, whether good or bad, triumphal or tragic, I ask that my responses always reflect a God-honoring attitude of optimism, faith, and love for You. Amen.

Walking in His Footsteps

I've laid down a pattern for you. What I've done, you do.
JOHN 13:15 MSG

As citizens of a fast-changing world, we face challenges that sometimes leave us feeling overworked, overcommitted, and overwhelmed. But God has different plans for us. He intends that we slow down long enough to praise Him and to glorify His Son.

Jesus loved you so much that He endured unspeakable humiliation and suffering for you. How will you respond to Christ's sacrifice? Will you take up your cross and follow Him (Luke 9:23) or will you choose another path? When you place your hopes squarely at the foot of the cross, and when you place Jesus squarely at the center of your life, you will be blessed.

Do you hope to fulfill God's purpose for your life? Do you seek a life of abundance and peace? Do you intend to be Christian, not just in name, but in deed? Then follow Christ. Follow Him by picking up your cross every day. When you do, you will quickly discover that Christ's love has the power to change everything, including you.

Jesus gives us hope because He keeps us company,
has a vision and knows the way we should go.
MAX LUCADO

A Prayer to End Your Day

Dear Jesus, because I am Your disciple, I will trust You, I will obey Your teachings, and I will share Your Good News. You have given me life abundant and life eternal, and I will trust Your promises tonight, tomorrow, and every day of my life. Amen.

30

God Is Our Refuge

God is our refuge and strength, a very present help in trouble.
PSALM 46:1 NKJV

All of us face difficult days, days when we become discouraged. And you are no exception. After all, you live in a world where expectations can be high and demands can be even higher.

If you find yourself enduring difficult circumstances, remember that God remains in His heaven. If you become discouraged with the direction of your life, turn your thoughts and prayers to Him. He is a God of possibility, not negativity. He will guide you through your difficulties and beyond them. And then, with a renewed spirit of optimism and hope, you can thank the Giver of all things good for gifts that are simply too numerous to count.

The Lord has promised that He will be your refuge and your strength. Your job, simply put, is to let Him.

Even in the winter, even in the midst of the storm, the sun is still there. Somewhere, up above the clouds, it still shines and warms and pulls at the life buried deep inside the brown branches and frozen earth. The sun is there! Spring will come.
GLORIA GAITHER

A Prayer to End Your Day

Dear heavenly Father, when I am troubled, You heal me. When I am afraid, You protect me. When I am discouraged, You lift me up. During difficult days, I will trust You. And whatever my circumstances, Lord, I thank You for Your blessings, for Your love, and for Your Son. Amen.

Beyond Envy

*Therefore, laying aside all malice, all deceit, hypocrisy,
envy, and all evil speaking, as newborn babes,
desire the pure milk of the word, that you may grow thereby.*

1 PETER 2:1–2 NKJV

Because we are frail, imperfect human beings, we are sometimes envious of others. But God's Word warns us that envy is sin. So we must guard ourselves against the natural tendency to feel resentment and jealousy when other folks experience good fortune.

It's worth noting that as believers, we have absolutely no reason to be envious of any people on earth. After all, as Christians we are already recipients of the greatest gift in all creation: God's grace. We have been promised the gift of eternal life through God's only begotten Son, and we must count that gift as our most precious possession.

So here's a simple suggestion that is guaranteed to bring you happiness, contentment, and a good night's sleep: fill your heart with God's love, God's promises, and God's Son. When you do, you'll leave no room in your heart for envy, hatred, bitterness, or regret.

What God asks, does, or requires of others is not my business; it is His.

KAY ARTHUR

A Prayer to End Your Day

Dear Lord, when I am envious of others, redirect my thoughts to the blessings I have received from You. Make me a thankful Christian, Father, and deliver me from envy tonight, tomorrow, and every day of my life. Amen.

Defeating Negativity

Do not judge others, and you will not be judged. Do not condemn others,
or it will all come back against you. Forgive others, and you will be forgiven.

LUKE 6:37 NLT

From experience, we know that it is easier to criticize than to correct; we understand that it is easier to find faults than solutions; and we realize that excessive criticism is usually destructive, not productive. Yet the urge to criticize others remains a powerful temptation for most of us. Our task, as obedient believers, is to break the twin habits of negative thinking and critical speech.

In the book of James, we are issued a clear warning: "Don't criticize one another, brothers" (4:11 HCSB). Undoubtedly, James understood the paralyzing power of chronic negativity, and so must we. Negativity is highly contagious: we give it to others who, in turn, give it back to us. Thankfully, this cycle can be broken by positive thoughts, heartfelt prayers, and encouraging words.

As you examine the quality of your own communications, can you honestly say that you're a booster not a critic? If so, keep up the good words. But if you're occasionally overwhelmed by negativity, and if you pass that negativity along to your neighbors, it's time for a mental housecleaning.

As a thoughtful Christian, you can use the transforming power of Christ's love to break the chains of negativity. And you should.

A Prayer to End Your Day

Dear Lord, let me be an expectant Christian. Let me expect the best from You, and let me look for the best in others. If I become discouraged, Father, turn my thoughts and my prayers to You. Let me trust You, Lord, to direct my life. And let me be Your faithful, hopeful, optimistic servant tonight, tomorrow, and every day of my life. Amen.

33

Put Faith above Feelings

Who is in charge of your emotions? Is it you, or have you formed the unfortunate habit of letting other people or troubling situations determine the quality and direction of your thoughts? If you're wise—and if you'd like to build a better life for yourself and your loved ones—you'll learn to control your emotions before your emotions control you.

Human emotions are highly variable, decidedly unpredictable, and often unreliable. Our emotions are like the weather, only far more fickle. So we must learn to live by faith, not by the ups and downs of our own emotional roller coasters.

Sometime soon, you will probably be gripped by a strong negative feeling. Distrust it. Reign it in. Test it. And turn it over to God. Your emotions will inevitably change; God will not. So trust Him completely and then watch as your negative feelings are transformed into positive thoughts and good deeds.

A Prayer to End Your Day

Heavenly Father, You are my strength and my refuge. When I am troubled, Lord, keep me steady, and when life is difficult, help me focus on Your protection, Your love, and Your Son. Amen.

34

Giving Thanks for Christ's Love

How much does Christ love us? More than we, as mere mortals, can comprehend. His love is perfect and steadfast. Even though we are fallible and wayward, the Good Shepherd cares for us still. Even though we have fallen far short of the Father's commandments, Christ loves us with a depth that is beyond our understanding. The sacrifice that Jesus made upon the cross was made for each of us, and His love endures to the edge of eternity and beyond.

Christ's love changes everything. When we accept His gift of grace, we are transformed, not only for today, but forever. Yes, Christ's love changes everything. May we invite Him into our hearts so that His love can then change everything in us.

A Prayer to End Your Day

Dear Jesus, my life has been changed forever by Your love and Your sacrifice. Tonight, I praise You; I honor You; and I give thanks for Your sacrifice. Thank You, Jesus, for Your priceless gift, and for Your compassion. You loved me first, Lord, and I will return Your love tonight, tomorrow, and forever. Amen.

35

God Can Handle It

It's a promise that is made over and over again in the Bible: whatever "it" is, God can handle it.

Life isn't always easy. Far from it! Sometimes life can be very, very difficult, indeed. But even when the storm clouds form overhead, even during our most stressful moments, we're protected by a loving heavenly Father.

When we're worried, God can reassure us; when we're sad, God can comfort us. When our hearts are broken, God is not just near; He is here. So we must lift our thoughts and prayers to Him. When we do, He will answer those prayers. Why? Because He is our shepherd, and He has promised to protect us now and forever. And the Lord always keeps His promises. Always.

A Prayer to End Your Day

Heavenly Father, You never leave or forsake me. You are always with me, protecting me and encouraging me. Whatever the future holds, I can be confident because I know that You are with me tonight, tomorrow, and forever. Amen.

Using God's Gifts

Based on the gift each one has received, use it to serve others,
as good managers of the varied grace of God.

1 PETER 4:10 HCSB

How do we thank God for the gifts He has given us? By using those gifts for the glory of His kingdom.

God has given you talents and opportunities that are uniquely yours. Are you willing to use your gifts in the way that God intends? And are you willing to summon the discipline that is required to develop your talents and hone your skills? That's precisely what God wants you to do, and that's precisely what you should desire for yourself.

As you seek to expand your talents, you will undoubtedly encounter stumbling blocks along the way, such as the fear of rejection or the fear of failure. When you do, don't stumble. Just continue to refine your skills and offer your services to God. When the time is right, He will use you—but it's up to you to be thoroughly prepared when He does.

You weren't an accident. You weren't mass produced. You aren't
an assembly-line product. You were deliberately planned, specifically
gifted, and lovingly positioned on the earth by the Master Craftsman.

MAX LUCADO

A Prayer to End Your Day

Heavenly Father, I praise You for Your priceless gifts. I give thanks for Your creation, for Your Son, and for the unique opportunities You have given me. Give me the courage to use my gifts for the glory of Your kingdom, now and forever. Amen.

Beyond Failure

For a righteous man may fall seven times and rise again.
PROVERBS 24:16 NKJV

The occasional disappointments and failures of life are inevitable. Such setbacks are simply the price that we must occasionally pay for our willingness to take risks as we follow our dreams. But even when we encounter bitter disappointments, we must never lose faith.

When we encounter difficult circumstances or life-altering obstacles, God stands ready to protect us. Our responsibility, of course, is to ask Him for protection. When we call upon Him in heartfelt prayer, He will answer—in His own time and according to His own plan—and He will heal our hearts. And while we are waiting for God's plans to unfold—and while we're waiting for His healing touch to restore us—we can be comforted in the knowledge that our Creator can overcome any obstacle, even if we cannot.

The enemy of our souls loves to taunt us with past failures,
wrongs, disappointments, disasters, and calamities.
And if we let him continue doing this, our life becomes
a long and dark tunnel, with very little light at the end.
CHARLES SWINDOLL

A Prayer to End Your Day

Dear Lord, even though I may be afraid of failure, give me the courage to try. Remind me that with You by my side, I really have nothing to fear. So I will live courageously, Father, as I place my faith in You. Amen.

A Worthy Disciple

*He has shown you, O mortal, what is good. And what does
the LORD require of you? To act justly and to love mercy
and to walk humbly with your God.*

MICAH 6:8 NIV

When Jesus addressed His disciples, He warned them that each one must, "take up his cross, and follow me" (Mark 8:34 KJV).

The disciples must have known exactly what the Master meant. In Jesus's day, prisoners were forced to carry their own crosses to the location where they would be put to death. Thus, Christ's message was clear: in order to follow Him, Christ's disciples must deny themselves and, instead, follow Him and trust Him completely. Nothing has changed since then.

How can we be good disciples? By sharing Christ's message, His mercy, and His love with those who cross our paths. Everywhere we look, or so it seems, the needs are great. And at every turn, it seems, so are the temptations. Still, our challenge is clear: we must love God, obey His commandments, trust His Son, and serve His children. When we place our Lord and His Son in their rightful place—first place—we will reap a bountiful spiritual harvest that will endure forever.

*Discipleship is a daily discipline:
we follow Jesus a step at a time, a day at a time.*

WARREN WIERSBE

A Prayer to End Your Day

Dear Lord, thank You for the gift of Your Son Jesus. Let me be a worthy disciple of Christ, and keep me mindful of His sacrifice. I will praise You always, Father, as I give thanks for Your Son, for His everlasting love, and for the gift of everlasting life. Amen.

The Peace That Passes All Understanding

The peace of God, which passeth all understanding,
shall keep your hearts and minds through Christ Jesus.
PHILIPPIANS 4:7 KJV

Peace. It's such a beautiful word. It conveys images of serenity, contentment, and freedom from the trials and tribulations of everyday existence. Peace means freedom from conflict, freedom from inner turmoil, and freedom from worry. Peace is such a beautiful concept that advertisers and marketers attempt to sell it with images of relaxed vacationers lounging on the beach or happy senior citizens celebrating on the golf course. But contrary to the implied claims of modern media, real peace, genuine peace, isn't for sale. At any price.

Have you discovered the genuine peace—the peace that passes human understanding—which can be yours through an intimate relationship with God's only begotten Son? Or are you still scurrying after the illusion of peace that the world promises but cannot deliver? If you've turned things over to Jesus, you'll be blessed now and forever. And you'll experience the peace that only He can give.

Deep within the center of the soul is a chamber of peace
where God lives and where, if we will enter it and quiet
all the other sounds, we can hear His gentle whisper.
LETTIE COWMAN

A Prayer to End Your Day

Heavenly Father, You give me a peace that the world can never offer. I thank You, Father, for blessings that are too numerous to count and too glorious to fully comprehend. Amen.

Perseverance and Hope

A well-lived life is like a marathon, not a sprint—it calls for preparation, determination, and, of course, lots of perseverance. As an example of perfect perseverance, we Christians need look no further than our Savior, Jesus Christ. Jesus finished what He began. Despite His suffering and despite the shame of the cross, He was steadfast in His faithfulness to God. We, too, must remain faithful, especially when times are tough.

Sometimes God may answer our prayers with silence, and when He does, we must patiently persevere.

Are you facing a difficult dilemma or a problem that seems impossible to solve? If so, remember this: whatever your problem, God can handle it. Your job is to keep persevering until He does.

A Prayer to End Your Day

Lord, when life is difficult, I am tempted to abandon hope. But You are my Shepherd, and I can draw strength from You. Let me trust You, Father, in good times and hard times. Let me persevere—even if my soul is troubled—and let me follow Your Son, Jesus, now and forever. Amen.

Finding Real Fulfillment

Everywhere we turn, or so it seems, the world promises fulfillment, contentment, and happiness. But the contentment that the world offers is fleeting and incomplete. Thankfully, the fulfillment that God offers is all encompassing and everlasting.

Sometimes, amid the inevitable hustle and bustle of life here on earth, we can forfeit—albeit temporarily—the joy of Christ as we wrestle with the challenges of daily living. Yet God's Word is clear:

fulfillment through Christ is available to all who seek it and claim it. Count yourself among that number. Seek first a personal, transforming relationship with Jesus, and then claim the joy, the fulfillment, and the spiritual abundance that the Shepherd offers His sheep.

A Prayer to End Your Day

Dear Lord, when I turn my thoughts and prayers to You, I feel peace and fulfillment. But sometimes, when I am distracted by the ups and downs of everyday life, fulfillment seems far away. Tonight when I go to sleep, and tomorrow morning when I wake up, let me trust Your will, let me be grateful for Your gifts, and let me accept Your peace. Amen.

-------- 42 --------

Finding Hope and Happiness

Do you sincerely want to be a happy Christian? Then you must set your mind and your heart upon God's love and His grace.

Happiness depends less upon our circumstances than upon our thoughts. When we turn our thoughts to the Lord, to His gifts, and to His glorious creation, we experience the joy that He intends for His children. But when we focus on the negative aspects of life, we suffer needlessly.

What does life have in store for you? A world full of possibilities (of course it's up to you to seize them), and God's promise of abundance (of course it's up to you to accept it). So as you embark upon the next phase of your journey, remember to celebrate the life that God has given you. Honor Him with your prayers, your words, your deeds, and your joy.

A Prayer to End Your Day

Dear Lord, I am thankful for all the blessings You have given me. Let me be a happy Christian, Father, as I share Your joy with friends, with family, and with the world. Amen.

In Difficult Times,
God Teaches and Leads

Leave inexperience behind, and you will live;
pursue the way of understanding.

PROVERBS 9:6 HCSB

Complete spiritual maturity is never achieved in a day or in a year or even in a lifetime. The journey toward spiritual maturity is an ongoing process that continues day by day, throughout every stage of life. Each chapter of life has its opportunities and its challenges, and if we're wise, we continue to seek God's guidance as the days and years unfold.

From time to time, all of us encounter circumstances that test our faith. We may be tempted to blame God or to rebel against Him. But the Bible reminds us that the trials of life should be viewed as opportunities for growth:

"Consider it a great joy, my brothers, whenever you experience various trials, knowing that the testing of your faith produces endurance. But endurance must do its complete work, so that you may be mature and complete, lacking nothing" (James 1:2–4 HCSB).

Have you recently encountered one of life's inevitable tests? If so, remember that God still has lessons that He intends to teach you. Your challenge, simply put, is to learn the lessons, to use them for spiritual growth, and to share your newfound insights with the world.

A Prayer to End Your Day

Dear Lord, when I open my heart to You, I am blessed. Show me Your way, Father, and let me grow in my faith tonight, tomorrow, and every day that I live. Amen.

Finding Contentment in a Discontented World

*I know what it is to be in need, and I know what it is to have plenty.
I have learned the secret of being content in any and every situation,
whether well fed or hungry, whether living in plenty or in want.
I can do all this through him who gives me strength.*

PHILIPPIANS 4:12–13 NIV

Where can we find the kind of contentment that Paul describes in Philippians 4? Is it a result of wealth or power or fame? Hardly. Genuine contentment is a gift from God to those who follow His commandments and accept His Son. When Christ dwells at the center of our families and our lives, contentment will belong to us just as surely as we belong to Him.

Do you want to experience happiness and spiritual abundance? If so, here are some things you should do: love God and His Son; depend upon God for strength; try, to the best of your abilities, to follow God's will; and strive to obey His Holy Word. When you do these things, you'll discover that happiness goes hand in hand with righteousness. The happiest people are not those who rebel against God; the happiest people are those who love God and obey His commandments.

Genuine contentment begins with God . . . and ends there.

A Prayer to End Your Day

Heavenly Father, when I turn my thoughts and prayers to You, I feel the peace and fulfillment that You intend for my life. You give me peace, Lord, when I draw close to You. Let me trust Your will and accept Your peace, tonight, tomorrow, and forever. Amen.

Infinite Possibilities

Are you afraid to ask the Lord to do big things in your life? If so, it's time to abandon your doubts and reclaim your faith in God's promises.

Ours is a God of infinite possibilities. But sometimes, because of limited faith and limited understanding, we wrongly assume that the Lord cannot or will not intervene in the affairs of mankind. Such assumptions are simply wrong.

God's Holy Word makes it clear: absolutely nothing is impossible for Him. And since the Bible means what it says, you can be comforted in the knowledge that the Creator of the universe can do miraculous things in your own life and in the lives of your loved ones. Your challenge, as a believer, is to take God at His word, and to expect the miraculous.

A Prayer to End Your Day

Dear God, nothing is impossible for You. Keep me mindful of Your strength. When I lose hope, give me faith; when others lose hope, let me remind them that Your power, like Your love, is infinite. Amen.

Focusing on God

All of us may find our courage tested by the inevitable disappointments and tragedies of life. Sometimes, our world is turned upside down by hardships and setbacks that we didn't anticipate. Trouble, it seems, is never too far from the front door.

When we focus upon our fears and our doubts, we may find many reasons to lie awake at night and fret about the uncertainties of the upcoming day. A better strategy, of course, is to focus not upon our fears, but instead upon our Lord.

God is as near as your next breath, and He is in control. He offers salvation to all His children, including you. God is your shield and your strength; you are His forever. So don't focus your thoughts on problems, obstacles, or hypothetical disasters that may never come to pass. Instead, trust God's plan and His eternal love for you. And remember: God is good, and He has the last word.

A Prayer to End Your Day

Your Word reminds me, Lord, that even when I experience difficult days, I need not fear because You are with me. Thank You, Lord, for a perfect love that casts out fear. Let me live courageously and faithfully every day of my life. Amen.

47

Don't Take Anger to Bed

Sometimes, anger is appropriate. Even Jesus became angry when confronted with the moneychangers in the temple. On occasion, you, like Jesus, will confront evil, and when you do, you may respond as He did: vigorously and without reservation. But more often than not, your frustrations will be of the more mundane variety.

As long as you live, you will face countless opportunities to lose your temper over small, relatively insignificant events: a traffic jam, a spilled cup of coffee, an inconsiderate comment, a broken promise. When you are tempted to lose your temper over the minor inconveniences of life, don't. Turn away from anger, hatred, bitterness, and regret. And be sure that you never take angry thoughts to bed with you.

Instead of complaining about your problems or fuming about your frustrations, turn them over to God. And leave them there.

A Prayer to End Your Day

Dear Lord, tonight I ask that You help me turn away from angry thoughts. Give me the wisdom and the strength to reject anger so that I may claim Your peace now and forever. Amen.

Focusing Your Thoughts and Prayers

Let your eyes look forward; fix your gaze straight ahead.
PROVERBS 4:25 HCSB

Tonight, as you prepare for sleep, you have yet another chance to celebrate the life that God has given you. It's also a chance to give thanks to the One who has offered you more blessings than you can possibly count. And it's another opportunity to direct your thoughts toward the very bright future that the Lord has in store for you.

So what's your focus tonight? Are you willing to focus your thoughts and energies on God's blessings and upon His will for your life? Or will you turn your thoughts to other things?

Tonight, why not focus on the joy that is rightfully yours in Christ? Why not take time to celebrate God's glorious creation? Why not trust your hopes instead of your fears? When you do, you will think optimistically about yourself and your world. And you'll sleep easier knowing that the Lord is your Shepherd and that you are protected.

*Occupy your minds with good thoughts, or your enemy
will fill them with bad ones; unoccupied they cannot be.*
SAINT THOMAS MORE

A Prayer to End Your Day

Dear Lord, You have blessed me in so many ways. Give me a grateful heart, Father. And tonight, let me focus my thoughts on You and Your incomparable gifts. Amen.

Trust God's Promises and Never Lose Hope

For you need endurance, so that after you have done God's will, you may receive what was promised.

HEBREWS 10:36 HCSB

God's Word contains promises upon which we, as Christians, can and must depend. The Bible is a priceless gift, a tool that God intends for us to use in every aspect of our lives; yet too many people keep their spiritual tool kits tightly closed and out of sight.

Are you tired? Discouraged? Fearful? Be comforted and trust the promises that God has made to you. Are you worried or anxious? Be confident in God's power. He will never desert you. Do you see a difficult future ahead? Be courageous and call upon God. He will protect you and then use you according to His purposes. Are you confused? Listen to the quiet voice of your heavenly Father. He is not a God of confusion. Talk with Him; listen to Him; trust Him, and trust His promises. He is steadfast, and He is your Protector tonight, tomorrow, and forever.

Don't let obstacles along the road to eternity shake your confidence in God's promises.

DAVID JEREMIAH

A Prayer to End Your Day

Dear Lord, Your Holy Word contains promises, and I will trust them. I will use the Bible as my guide, and I will trust You, Lord, to speak to me through Your Holy Spirit and through Your Holy Word, tonight, tomorrow, and forever. Amen.

The Promise of Eternal Life

Because I live, you will live also.
JOHN 14:19 NASB

Ours is not a distant God. Ours is a God who understands—far better than we ever could—the essence of what it means to be human. How marvelous it is that God became a man and walked among us. Had He not chosen to do so, we might feel removed from a distant Creator.

The Lord understands our hopes, our fears, and our temptations. He understands what it means to be angry and what it costs to forgive. He knows the heart, the conscience, and the soul of every person who has ever lived, including you. And God has a plan of salvation that is intended for you. Accept it. Accept God's gift through the person of His Son Christ Jesus, and then rest assured: God walked among us so that you might have eternal life. Amazing though it may seem, He did it for you.

Teach us to set our hopes on heaven, to hold firmly
to the promise of eternal life, so that we can
withstand the struggles and storms of this world.
MAX LUCADO

A Prayer to End Your Day

I know, Lord, that this world is not my home; I am only here for a brief while. And You have given me the priceless gift of eternal life through Your Son Jesus. Keep the hope of heaven fresh in my heart, Father, and while I am in this world, help me to pass through it with faith in my heart and praise on my lips for You. Amen.

Seek Fellowship

*For where two or three are gathered together in My name,
I am there among them.*

MATTHEW 18:20 HCSB

You can guard your heart and improve your life by becoming an active participant in a local church. When you make a habit of spending time with likeminded believers, you'll enhance your own life and theirs. Plus, you'll be protecting yourself (and them) against the inevitable distractions, frustrations, and temptations that have become so commonplace in modern society.

Are you an active member of a vibrant local fellowship? Are you a builder of bridges inside the four walls of your church and outside it? Do you contribute to God's glory by contributing your time and your talents to a close-knit band of believers? Hopefully so. The fellowship of believers is intended to be a powerful tool for spreading God's Good News and uplifting His children. God intends for you to be a fully contributing member of that fellowship. Your intentions should be the same.

*Be united with other Christians. A wall with loose bricks is not good.
The bricks must be cemented together.*

CORRIE TEN BOOM

A Prayer to End Your Day

Heavenly Father, You have given me a community of supporters called the church. Let our fellowship be a reflection of the love we feel for each other and the love we feel for You. Amen.

Giving Thanks to the Creator

In everything give thanks; for this is the will of God in Christ Jesus for you.
1 Thessalonians 5:18 NKJV

Most of us have been blessed beyond measure, but sometimes, as busy people living in a demanding world, we are sometimes slow to count our gifts and even slower to give thanks to the Giver. Our blessings include life and health, family and friends, freedom and possessions—for starters. And those blessings are multiplied when we share them with others.

Psalm 145 makes this promise: "The Lord is gracious and compassionate, slow to anger and rich in love. The Lord is good to all; he has compassion on all he has made" (vv. 8–9 NIV).

God loves us; He cares for us; He has a plan for each of us; and He has offered us the gift of eternal life through His Son. Considering all the things that the Lord has done, we owe it to Him—and to ourselves—to slow down many times each day and offer our thanks. His grace is everlasting; our thanks should be too.

*We ought to give thanks for all fortune: if it is good,
because it is good, if bad, because it works in us patience, humility,
the contempt of this world and the hope of our eternal country.*
C. S. Lewis

A Prayer to End Your Day

Heavenly Father, Your gifts are greater than I can imagine. Let me end each day—and begin each day—with thanksgiving in my heart and praise on my lips. Thank You for the gift of Your Son and for the promise of eternal life. Let me share the joyous news of Jesus Christ, and let my life be a testimony to His love and His grace. Amen.

The Right Kind of Fear

The fear of the LORD is the beginning of knowledge.
PROVERBS 1:7 HCSB

Do you have a healthy, fearful respect for God's power? Hopefully so. After all, God's Word teaches us that the fear of the Lord is the beginning of knowledge. When you fear the Creator—and when you honor Him by obeying His commandments—you will receive God's approval and His blessings.

Is faithfulness to the Lord your highest priority? Have you given His Son your heart, your soul, your talents, and your time? The answer to these questions will determine how you prioritize your days and organize your life. So tonight, as you reflect on day that has passed, and as you consider the opportunities that will inevitably present themselves in the future, remember this: until you acquire a healthy fear of God's power, your education is incomplete, and so, for that matter, is your faith.

If a person fears God, he or she has no reason
to fear anything else. On the other hand,
if a person does not fear God, then fear becomes a way of life.
BETH MOORE

A Prayer to End Your Day

Dear Lord, let my greatest fear be the fear of displeasing You. I will strive, Father, to obey Your commandments and seek Your will every day of my life. Amen.

He Is Sufficient

The LORD is my rock, my fortress, and my deliverer.
PSALM 18:2 HCSB

It is easy to become overwhelmed by the demands of everyday life, but if you're a faithful follower of the One from Galilee, you need never be overwhelmed. Why? Because God's love is sufficient to meet your needs. Whatever dangers you may face, whatever heartbreaks you must endure, God is with you, and He stands ready to comfort you and to heal you.

The Psalmist wrote, "Weeping may endure for a night, but joy comes in the morning" (Psalm 30:5 NKJV). But when we are suffering, the morning may seem very far away. It is not. God promises that He is "near to those who have a broken heart" (Psalm 34:18).

If you are experiencing the intense pain of a recent loss, or if you are still mourning a loss from long ago, perhaps you are now ready to begin the next stage of your journey with God. If so, be mindful of this fact: your Father in heaven is sufficient to meet any challenge, including yours.

The last and greatest lesson that the soul has to learn is the fact that God, and God alone, is enough for all its needs. This is the crowning discovery of our whole Christian life: God is enough!
HANNAH WHITALL SMITH

A Prayer to End Your Day

Lord, You have promised never to leave me or forsake me. You are always with me, Father, protecting me and encouraging me. I thank You for Your love and for Your strength. Tonight, I will remind myself, yet again, that You are sufficient to meet my every need, now and forever. Amen.

Put God in His Rightful Place

Do not have other gods besides Me.
EXODUS 20:3 HCSB

As you think about the nature of your relationship with God, remember this: you will *always* have some type of relationship with Him—it is inevitable that your life *must* be lived in relationship to God. The question is not *if* you will have a relationship with Him; the burning question is whether that relationship will be one that seeks to honor Him . . . or not.

In the book of Exodus, God warns that we should put no gods before Him. Yet all too often, we place our Lord in second, third, or fourth place as we focus on other things. When we place our desires for possessions and status above our love for God—or when we yield to the countless distractions that surround us—we forfeit the peace that might otherwise be ours.

In the wilderness, Satan offered Jesus earthly power and unimaginable riches, but Jesus refused. Instead, He chose to worship His heavenly Father. We must do likewise by putting God first and worshiping Him only. God must come first. Always first.

Jesus Christ is the first and last, author and finisher, beginning and end, alpha and omega, and by Him all other things hold together. He must be first or nothing. God never comes next!
VANCE HAVNER

A Prayer to End Your Day

Dear Lord, Your love is eternal and Your laws are everlasting. Tonight, I invite You to reign over every corner of my heart. I understand the need to place You first in every aspect of my life. You have blessed me beyond measure, Father, and I will praise You with my prayers, with my testimony, and with my service. Amen.

Guard Your Heart and Mind

God loves you; He cares for you; and He wants the very best for you. The Lord knows that your adversary is near, and He wants you to guard against distractions and temptations that can do you harm. In other words, God wants you to guard your heart.

Every day and every night, you're faced with an array of choices—more choices than you can count. You can do the right thing, or not. You can be prudent, or not. You can be humble, kind, and obedient. Or not.

From morning until night, the world offers you countless opportunities to let down your guard and, by doing so, to make needless mistakes that may injure you and your loved ones. So be watchful. Guard your heart by giving it to your heavenly Father; it is safe with Him.

A Prayer to End Your Day

Dear Lord, I will guard my heart against the distractions and temptations that are woven into the fabric of modern life. I will focus, instead, upon Your love, Your blessings, and Your Son. Amen.

Finding Strength for the Journey

God's love and support never changes. From the cradle to the grave, God has promised to give you the strength to meet any challenge. God has promised to lift you up and guide your steps if you let Him. God has promised that when you entrust your life to Him completely and without reservation, He will give you the courage to face any trial and the wisdom to live in His righteousness.

God uplifts those who turn their hearts and prayers to Him. Will you count yourself among that number? Will you accept

God's peace and wear God's armor against the distractions and discouragements of our dangerous world? If you do, you can live courageously and optimistically, knowing that the same Creator who brought light out of darkness can plant light and hope in your heart too.

A Prayer to End Your Day

Lord, sometimes life is difficult. Sometimes I am worried, weary, or heartbroken. But when I lift my eyes to You, Father, You strengthen me. When I am weak, You lift me up. Tonight, I turn to You, Lord, for my strength, for my hope, and my eternal salvation. Amen.

58

Beyond Grief

If you're experiencing the pains of a significant loss, God's promises offer comfort. And if you'd like to experience God's peace, Bible study can help provide it.

Warren Wiersbe observed, "When the child of God looks into the Word of God, he sees the Son of God. And, he is transformed by the Spirit of God to share in the glory of God." God's Holy Word is, indeed, a life-changing, spirit-lifting, one-of-a-kind treasure. And it's up to you—and only you—to use it that way.

Jonathan Edwards advised, "Be assiduous in reading the Holy Scriptures. This is the fountain whence all knowledge in divinity must be derived. Therefore let not this treasure lie by you neglected." God's Holy Word is, indeed, a priceless treasure. Handle it with care, but more importantly, handle it every day, especially when you're recovering from a painful loss.

A Prayer to End Your Day

Dear Lord, Your Word promises that You will not give me more than I can bear; You have promised to lift me out of grief and despair. Tonight, Lord, I pray for those who mourn, and I thank You for sustaining us in our days of sorrow. Amen.

Values Matter

Do not conform to the pattern of this world, but be transformed by the renewing of your mind. Then you will be able to test and approve what God's will is–his good, pleasing and perfect will.
ROMANS 12:2 NIV

It's important to know where we stand and what we stand for. It's imperative to establish values and live by them—talking about them isn't enough.

God's Word teaches us how to live; it tells us what to do and what not to do. As Christians we are called to walk with God's Son and to obey God's commandments. But, we live in a world that presents us with many temptations, each of which has the potential to distract us or destroy us.

Charles Swindoll correctly observed, "Nothing speaks louder or more powerfully than a life of integrity." Wise men and women agree. So as you establish the set of values that you'll live by—and lead by—make the Bible your guidebook. When you do, you'll be protected and you'll be blessed.

When you live in the light of eternity, your values change.
RICK WARREN

A Prayer to End Your Day

Heavenly Father, it is so much easier to speak of the righteous life than it is to live it. Let me live righteously; let my actions be consistent with my beliefs; and let every step that I take reflect Your truth. Amen.

Beyond Worry

Therefore do not worry about tomorrow, for tomorrow will worry about its own things. Sufficient for the day is its own trouble.

MATTHEW 6:34 NKJV

Because we are imperfect human beings, we worry. Even though we are Christians who have been given the assurance of salvation—even though we are Christians who have received the promise of God's love and protection—we find ourselves fretting over the countless details of everyday life. Jesus understood our concerns when he spoke the reassuring words found in the sixth chapter of Matthew: "Therefore I tell you, do not worry about your life . . ." (v. 25 NIV).

Billy Graham once observed, "Anxiety is the natural result when our hopes are centered on anything short of God and His will for us." Pastor Graham was right. When we focus on the world and its problems, we become anxious. When we focus on the Lord and His love for us, we find peace.

As you consider God's promises, remember that He still sits in His heaven and you are His beloved child. Then, perhaps, you will worry a little less and trust God a little more, and that's as it should be because God is trustworthy . . . and you are protected.

We are not called to be burden-bearers, but cross-bearers and light-bearers. We must cast our burdens on the Lord.

CORRIE TEN BOOM

A Prayer to End Your Day

Forgive me, Lord, when I worry. Worry reflects a lack of trust in You. Help me to work, Lord, and not to worry. And keep me mindful, Father, that nothing, absolutely nothing, will happen tonight—or tomorrow—that You and I cannot handle together. Amen.

He Cares for You

*Therefore humble yourselves under the mighty hand of God,
that He may exalt you at the proper time,
casting all your anxiety on Him, because He cares for you.*
1 PETER 5:6–7 NASB

Do the demands of everyday life seem overwhelming? If so, you must rely, not only upon your own resources, but also upon the promises of your Father in heaven. God has promised to lift you up and guide your steps if you let Him. And God has promised that when you entrust your life to Him completely and without reservation, He will give you the strength to meet any challenge, the courage to face any trial, and the wisdom to live in His righteousness. These promises should give you great comfort.

In a world brimming with dangers and distractions, God is the ultimate armor. In a world saturated with misleading messages, God's Word is the ultimate truth. In a world filled with frustrations, God's Son offers the ultimate peace.

So as you prepare for sleep, remember that your heavenly Father never leaves you, not even for a moment. He's always available, always ready to listen, always ready to lead. When you make a habit of talking to Him every day and every night, you'll have less to worry about and more to celebrate.

Himself with the care and keeping of you.
HANNAH WHITALL SMITH

A Prayer to End Your Day

Heavenly Father, thank You for Your comfort. You lift me up when I am disappointed. You protect me in times of trouble. You are with me when I grieve. Tonight, I will be mindful of Your love, Your wisdom, and Your grace. Amen.

Trust God's Timetable

He has made everything appropriate in its time.
He has also put eternity in their hearts, but man cannot discover
the work God has done from beginning to end.

ECCLESIASTES 3:11 HCSB

If you seek to be a person of faith, you must learn to trust God's timing. You will be sorely tempted, however, to do otherwise. If you're like most people, you're in a hurry. You know precisely what you want, and you know precisely when you want it: as soon as possible. Because your time on earth is limited, you may feel a sense of urgency. God does not. There is no panic in heaven.

Our heavenly Father, in His infinite wisdom, operates according to His own timetable, not ours. He has plans that we cannot see and purposes that we cannot know. He has created a world that unfolds according to His own schedule. Thank goodness! After all, He is omniscient; He is trustworthy; and He knows what's best for us.

If you've been waiting impatiently for the Lord to answer your prayers, it's time to put a stop to all that needless worry. You can be sure that God will answer your prayers when the time is right. You job is to keep praying—and working—until He does.

God knows not only what we need but also when we need it.
His timing is always perfect.

ELISABETH ELLIOT

A Prayer to End Your Day

Dear Lord, Your timing may not be my timing, but Your timing is always right for me. You are my Father, and You have a plan for my life that is grander than I can imagine. When I am impatient, remind me that You are never early or late. You are always on time, Lord, so I will trust You always. Amen.

It's Okay to Step Back; It's Okay to Slow Down

Don't burn out; keep yourselves fueled and aflame. Be alert servants of the Master, cheerfully expectant. Don't quit in hard times; pray all the harder.
ROMANS 12:11-12 MSG

Are you one of those people who is simply too busy for your own good? If so, you're doing everybody a disservice by heaping needless stresses upon yourself and your loved ones.

As you consider your priorities, remember that time with God is paramount. You owe it to yourself to spend time with your Creator, seeking His guidance and studying His Word. Those quiet moments of prayer and meditation are invaluable. When you let God help you organize your life, you'll find that He'll give you the time and the tools do the most important tasks on your to-do list. And what about all those less important things on your list? Perhaps they're best left undone.

Tonight, as a gift to yourself, to your family, and to your world, take time to reconsider your priorities. And while you're at it, be sure to focus on your highest priority: your relationship with God. Allow the Lord to preside over every aspect of your life. It's the best way to live and the surest path to peace tonight, tomorrow, and forever.

A Prayer to End Your Day

Dear Lord, when the quickening pace of life leaves me with little time for worship or for praise, help me reorder my priorities. When the demands of the day leave me distracted and discouraged, let me turn to Jesus for the peace that only He can give. And then, when I have accepted the spiritual abundance that is mine through Christ, let me share His message and His love with all who cross my path. Amen.

God's Infinite Love

The LORD's lovingkindnesses indeed never cease, for His compassions never fail. They are new every morning. Great is Your faithfulness.
LAMENTATIONS 3:22-23 NASB

The line from the children's song is reassuring and familiar: "Jesus loves me! this I know, for the Bible tells me so. Little ones to Him belong, they are weak but He is strong." That message applies to kids of all ages: we are all indeed weak, but we worship a mighty God who meets our needs and answers our prayers.

Are you in the midst of adversity, or are you enduring an unfortunate situation that you didn't initiate and don't fully understand? If so, turn to God for strength. The Bible promises that you can do all things through the power of our risen Savior, Jesus Christ. Your challenge, then, is clear. You must place Christ where He belongs: at the very center of your life. When you do, you will discover that, yes, Jesus loves you and that, yes, He will give you direction and strength if you ask for it in His name.

*There is no limit to God. There is no limit to His power.
There is no limit to His love. There is no limit to His mercy.*
BILLY GRAHAM

A Prayer to End Your Day

Thank You, Lord, for Your love. Tonight, as I pause and reflect upon Your gifts, I understand the need to place You first in every aspect of my life. Your love is boundless, infinite, and eternal, and I praise You, Father, for that priceless gift. Amen.

Keep Celebrating

The Psalm 118 reminds us that every day is a cause for celebration. Each day is presented to us fresh and clean at midnight, free of charge. But we must beware: every day is a non-renewable resource—once it's gone, it's gone forever. Our responsibility, of course, is to use our time here on earth in the service of our Lord.

Every day is a priceless gift from above. Every day the Lord offers us yet another opportunity to serve Him with smiling faces and willing hands. When we do our part, He inevitably does His part, and miracles happen.

The Lord has promised to bless you and keep you, now and forever. So don't wait for birthdays or holidays. Make each day an exciting adventure. And while you're at it, take time to thank God for His blessings. He deserves your gratitude, and you deserve the joy of expressing it.

A Prayer to End Your Day

Dear Lord, as I come to the end of this day, I am mindful that every day is a gift from You. Thank You, Father, for the gift of life here on earth, and for the priceless gift of eternal life. Tonight, tomorrow, and every day of my life, I ask for the wisdom to celebrate Your blessings and share them with the world. Amen.

Avoiding the Trap of Pessimism

Pessimism is intellectual poison. And negativity has the power to harm your heart if you let it. So if you've allowed negative thoughts to creep into your mind and heart, here's your assignment: start spending more time thinking about your blessings and less time fretting about your problems.

Every day is a gift from God, filled to the brim with possibilities. But persistent pessimistic thoughts can rob you of the energy you need to accomplish the most important tasks on your to-do list. So as you survey the landscape of your life, be careful to direct your thoughts toward things positive. And while you're at it, take time to thank the Giver of all things good for gifts that are, in truth, far too numerous to count.

A Prayer to End Your Day

Dear Lord, keep me mindful that negativity is a trap. So whenever I feel discouraged or fearful, I pray for the wisdom to replace my doubts with faith. Let me expect the best from You, and let me look for the best in others tonight, tomorrow, and every day of my life. Amen.

67

Cheerful Christianity

Christ promises us lives of abundance and joy, but He does not force His joy upon us. We must claim His joy for ourselves, and when we do, Jesus, in turn, fills our spirits with His power and His love.

So how can we receive from Christ the joy that is rightfully ours? By giving Him what is rightfully His: our hearts and our souls.

When we earnestly commit ourselves to the Savior of mankind, and when we place Jesus at the center of our lives, and when we trust Him as our personal Savior, He will transform us, not just for today, but for all eternity. Then we, as God's children, can share Christ's joy and His message with a world that needs both.

A Prayer to End Your Day

Dear Lord, as I come to the end of this day, I realize that You have given me so many reasons to celebrate. Let me be a joyful Christian who is quick to smile and slow to anger. And let me share Your goodness with others so that Your love might shine in me and through me. Amen.

Accepting the Past, Embracing the Future

Do not remember the former things, nor consider the things of old. Behold, I will do a new thing.

ISAIAH 43:18–19 NKJV

Some of life's greatest roadblocks are not the ones we see through the windshield; they are, instead, the roadblocks that seem to fill the rearview mirror. Instead of focusing our thoughts and energies on the opportunities ahead of us, we allow painful memories to fill our minds, to hijack our emotions and to sap our strength. We simply can't seem to let go of our pain, so we relive it again and again, with predictably unfortunate consequences. Thankfully, God has other plans.

God's Word instructs us to focus on the future, not the past. When we do, we free ourselves of poisonous emotions such as bitterness, regret, and hate. But that's not all. We also free ourselves to channel our energies and invest our time in endeavors that can improve our lives and make the world a better place.

If you've had trouble making peace with your past, ask God to help you accept the past and embrace the future. It's the logical way to think and the best way to live.

You must learn, you must let God teach you, that the only way to get rid of your past is to make a future out of it. God will waste nothing.

PHILLIPS BROOKS

A Prayer to End Your Day

Dear Lord, help me live in the present, not the past. When I am bitter or resentful, I do not feel the peace that You intend for me to experience. So help me accept the past, treasure the present, and look forward to a future with You that is eternally bright. Amen.

The Greatest of These Is Love

But now faith, hope, love, abide these three;
but the greatest of these is love.

1 CORINTHIANS 13:13 NASB

We are commanded (not advised, not encouraged; we are *commanded!*) to love one another just as Christ loved us (John 13:34). God is love, and He intends that we share His love with the world. But He won't force us to be loving and kind. He places that responsibility squarely on our shoulders.

Love, like everything else in this world, begins and ends with the Lord, but the middle part belongs to us. The Creator gives each of us the opportunity to be kind, to be courteous, and to be loving. He gives each of us the chance to obey the Golden Rule *or* to make up our own rules as we go. If we obey God's instructions, we're secure, but if we do otherwise, we suffer.

Christ's words are clear: "'Love the Lord your God with all your heart and with all your soul and with all your mind.' This is the first and greatest commandment. And the second is like it: 'Love your neighbor as yourself.' All the Law and the Prophets hang on these two commandments" (Matthew 22:37–40 NIV).

We are commanded to love the One who first loved us and then to share His love with the world. And the next move is always ours.

Where Love is, God is. He that dwells in Love dwells in God.

HENRY DRUMMOND

A Prayer to End Your Day

Lord, love is Your commandment. Help me always to remember that the gift of love is a precious gift indeed. Let me nurture love and treasure it, now and forever. Amen.

Let God Guide the Way

The true children of God are those who let God's Spirit lead them.
ROMANS 8:14 NCV

The Bible promises that God will guide you if you let Him. Your job, of course, is to let Him. But sometimes you will be tempted to do otherwise. Sometimes you'll be tempted to go along with the crowd; other times you'll be tempted to do things your way, not God's way. When you feel those temptations, resist them.

Corrie ten Boom observed, "God's guidance is even more important than common sense. I can declare that the deepest darkness is outshone by the light of Jesus." These words remind us that life is best lived when we seek the Lord's direction in every circumstance and in every stage of life.

Our heavenly Father has many ways to make Himself known. Our challenge is to make ourselves open to His instruction. So if you're unsure of your next step, trust God's promises and talk to Him often. When you do, He'll guide your steps tonight, tomorrow, and every day after that.

When there is perplexity there is always guidance—
not always at the moment we ask, but in good time,
which is God's time. There is no need to fret and stew.
ELISABETH ELLIOT

A Prayer to End Your Day

Dear Lord, I know that You have a plan for my life. Tonight, as I prepare for sleep, I can be at peace, knowing that when I trust Your plan, I am eternally blessed. Amen.

Consider the Possibilities

For nothing will be impossible with God.
LUKE 1:37 HCSB

Are you afraid to ask God to do big things—or to make big changes—in your life? Is your faith threadbare and worn? If so, it's time to abandon your doubts and reclaim your faith in God's promises.

Ours is a God of infinite possibilities. But sometimes, because of limited faith and limited understanding, we wrongly assume that God cannot or will not intervene in the affairs of mankind. Such assumptions are simply wrong.

God's Holy Word makes it clear: absolutely nothing is impossible for the Lord. And since the Bible means what it says, you can be comforted in the knowledge that the Creator of the universe can do miraculous things in your own life and in the lives of your loved ones. Your challenge, as a believer, is to take God at His word, and to expect the miraculous.

*Beware in your prayers, above everything else,
of limiting God, not only by unbelief, but by fancying
that you know what He can do. Expect unexpected things.*
ANDREW MURRAY

A Prayer to End Your Day

Dear Lord, give me the courage to dream and the faithfulness to trust in Your perfect plan for my life. Tonight, Father, I will be mindful that nothing is impossible for You. Absolutely nothing. Amen.

True Peace and Enduring Hope

You, LORD, give true peace to those who
depend on you, because they trust you.

ISAIAH 26:3 NCV

Sometimes hope is a perishable commodity. Despite God's promises, despite Christ's love, and despite our countless blessings, we are frail human beings who can still lose hope from time to time. When the challenges and pressures of everyday life threaten to overwhelm us, we may convince ourselves that the future holds little promise—and we may allow our fears to eclipse our dreams.

When hope seems to be in short supply, there is a source to which we can turn in order to restore our perspective and our strength. That source is God. When we lift our prayers to the Creator, we avail ourselves of God's power, God's wisdom, and God's love. And when we allow God's Son to reign over our hearts, we are transformed, not just for a day, but for all eternity.

Are you looking for a renewed sense of hope? If so, it's time to entrust your future to the Lord. When you do, you'll discover that hope is not only highly perishable, but that it is also readily renewable: one day—and one moment—at a time.

Never yield to gloomy anticipation. Place your hope
and confidence in God. He has no record of failure.

LETTIE COWMAN

A Prayer to End Your Day

Dear Lord, sometimes life can be challenging, and sometimes bad things happen. If I become discouraged, I will turn to You. If I am afraid, I will seek strength in You. In every aspect of my life, I will trust You. You are my Father, and I will place my hope, my trust, and my faith in You. Amen.

Perspective for Today

Don't turn your back on wisdom, for she will protect you.
Love her, and she will guard you.

PROVERBS 4:6 NLT

Sometimes, amid the demands of daily life, we lose perspective. Life seems out of balance, and the pressures of everyday living seem overwhelming. What's needed is a fresh perspective, a restored sense of balance, and God.

If a temporary loss of perspective has left you worried, exhausted, or both, it's time to readjust your thought patterns. Negative thoughts are habit-forming; thankfully, so are positive ones. With practice, you can form the habit of focusing on God's priorities and your possibilities. When you do, you'll soon discover that you will spend less time fretting about your challenges and more time praising God for His gifts.

When you call upon the Lord and prayerfully seek His will, He will give you wisdom and perspective. When you make God's priorities your priorities, He will direct your steps and calm your fears. So tonight, tomorrow, and every day thereafter, pray for a sense of balance and perspective. And remember: your thoughts are intensely powerful things, so handle them with care.

A Prayer to End Your Day

Dear Lord, when the pace of my life becomes frantic, slow me down and give me perspective. Give me the wisdom to realize that the problems of today are only temporary but that Your love is eternal. When I become discouraged, keep me steady and sure as I trust Your promises and follow in the footsteps of Your Son. Amen.

When It's Time for a Fresh Start

The LORD says, "Forget what happened before,
and do not think about the past. Look at the new thing
I am going to do. It is already happening. Don't you see it?
I will make a road in the desert and rivers in the dry land."

ISAIAH 43:18–19 NCV

Our heavenly Father has the power to make all things new. When we go to Him with sincere hearts and willing hands, He renews our spirits and redirects our steps.

Are you searching for a new path? If so, the Lord is waiting patiently to give you a fresh start. He's prepared to help you change your thoughts, rearrange your priorities and transform your life. But it doesn't stop there. He's also made a standing offer to forgive your sins, to forget your failings, and to protect you throughout all eternity. Your only responsibility is to ask for His help and to follow His Son.

Are you ready for a new beginning? If so, start now. Make God your partner in every endeavor. He can make all things new, including you.

God is not running an antique shop! He is making all things new!
VANCE HAVNER

A Prayer to End Your Day

Dear Lord, You have plans for me: plans for renewal, plans for transformation, plans for a new beginning. I will seek Your guidance and entrust my future to You, tonight, tomorrow, and every day of my life. Amen.

Answering the Call

*I urge you who have been chosen by God
to live up to the life to which God called you.*

EPHESIANS 4:1 NCV

God is calling you to follow a specific path that He has chosen for your life. And it is vitally important that you heed that call. Otherwise, your talents and opportunities may go unused.

Have you already heard God's call? And are you pursuing it with vigor? If so, you're both fortunate and wise. But if you have not yet discovered what God intends for you to do with your life, keep searching and keep praying until you discover why the Creator put you here.

Remember: God has important work for you to do—work that no one else on earth can accomplish but you. The Creator has placed you in particular location, amid particular people, with unique opportunities to serve. And He has given you all the tools you need to succeed. So listen for His voice, watch for His signs, and prepare yourself for the call that is sure to come.

*There's some task which the God of all the universe, the great Creator
has for you to do, and which will remain undone and incomplete,
until by faith and obedience, you step into the will of God.*

ALAN REDPATH

A Prayer to End Your Day

Heavenly Father, You have called me, and I acknowledge that calling. I will study Your Word and seek Your guidance. Give me the wisdom to know Your will for my life and the courage to follow wherever You may lead me. Amen.

Experiencing Silence

Jesus understood the importance of silence. He spent precious hours alone with God, and so should we. But with our busy schedules, we're tempted to rush from place to place, checking smart phones along the way, leaving no time to contemplate spiritual matters.

You live in a noisy world, a complicated society where sights and sounds surround you and silence is in short supply. Everywhere you turn, or so it seems, the media seeks to grab your attention and hijack your thoughts.

Whether you realize it or not, you need quiet, uninterrupted time alone with God. You need to be still and listen for His voice. Your Creator has important plans for you, and He has important lessons He intends for you to learn. You owe it to Him—and to yourself—to listen and to learn in silence.

A Prayer to End Your Day

Dear Lord, help me remember the importance of silence. Tonight and every night, help me treasure those quiet moments when I can sense Your presence and Your love. Amen.

Let Jesus Guide the Way

Thomas Brooks spoke for believers of every generation when he observed, "Christ is the sun, and all the watches of our lives should be set by the dial of his motion." Christ, indeed, is the ultimate savior of mankind and the personal savior of those who believe in Him. As his servants, we should place Him at the very center of our lives. And every day that God gives us breath, we should share Christ's love and His message with a world that needs both.

Our circumstances change, and the world keeps changing

too. But Jesus does not change. Even when the world seems to be trembling between our feet, Jesus remains the spiritual bedrock that cannot be moved.

You are the recipient of Christ's love. Accept it enthusiastically and share it passionately. Jesus deserves your undivided attention. And when you give it to Him, you'll be forever grateful that you did.

A Prayer to End Your Day

Dear Jesus, You are my Savior and my protector. Give me the courage to trust You completely. Tonight, tomorrow, and every day of my life I will praise You, I will honor You, and I will strive to follow in Your footsteps. Amen.

78

The Right Priorities

Have you asked God to help prioritize Your life? Have you asked Him for guidance and for the courage to do the things that you know need to be done? If so, then you're continually inviting your Creator to reveal Himself in a variety of ways. As a follower of Christ, you should do no less.

When you make God's priorities your priorities, you will receive God's abundance and His peace. When you make God a full partner in every aspect of your life, He will lead you along the proper path: His path. When you allow God to reign over your heart, He will honor you with spiritual blessings that are simply too numerous to count.

So as you make plans for tomorrow, make God's will your ultimate priority. When you do, every other priority will have a tendency to fall neatly into place.

A Prayer to End Your Day

Lord, tomorrow let Your priorities be my priorities. Let Your will be my will. Let Your Word be my guide, and let me grow in faith and in wisdom every day of my life. Amen.

Discovering God's Plans

*It is God who is at work in you, both to will
and to work for His good pleasure.*

PHILIPPIANS 2:13 NASB

God has a plan for the world, and He has a plan for you. He has given you talents, opportunities, and time. And He knows that His plan for you is best. But the Lord won't force His plans upon you. He's given you free will, the ability to make choices on your own. The totality of those choices will determine how well you fulfill God's calling.

Sometimes God makes Himself know in obvious ways, but more often His guidance is subtle. So we must pray often and listen carefully if we wish to hear His voice.

If you're serious about discovering God's plan for your life—or rediscovering it—start spending quiet time with Him. Ask Him for direction. Pray for clarity. And be watchful for His signs. The more time you spend with the Lord, the sooner the answers will come.

*God has a plan for the life of every Christian.
Every circumstance, every turn of destiny,
all things work together for your good and for His glory.*

BILLY GRAHAM

A Prayer to End Your Day

Dear Lord, You created me for a reason. Give me the wisdom to follow Your direction on my life's journey. Let me do Your work here on earth by seeking Your will and living it, knowing that when I trust in You, Father, I am eternally blessed. Amen.

The Shepherd Cares for You

My cup runs over. Surely goodness and mercy shall follow me all the days of my life; and I will dwell in the house of the LORD forever.

PSALM 23:5–6 NKJV

"The Lord is my Shepherd." These familiar words remind us that God is always with us, and that He protects us in every stage, and in every phase of life. When we entrust our hearts and our days to the One who created us, we experience abundance through the grace and sacrifice of His Son. In every circumstance, during times of wealth or times of want, God has promised to provide for our spiritual, emotional, and material needs. When we turn our concerns over to Him, He fulfills that promise.

God can manage every situation, and He can give you the spiritual abundance you so earnestly desire. Your responsibility is to let Him. When you do, you will receive the love and the abundance that He has promised. So tonight, as you give thanks to your heavenly Father, trust Him completely, and then claim the joy, the peace, and the spiritual abundance that the Shepherd offers His sheep.

God is the giver, and we are the receivers. And His richest gifts are bestowed not upon those who do the greatest things, but upon those who accept His abundance and His grace.

HANNAH WHITALL SMITH

A Prayer to End Your Day

Dear Lord, I thank You for the abundant life that is mine through Christ Jesus. Tonight, I ask You to guide me according to Your will, and help me to be a worthy servant in all that I say and do. Give me courage, Lord, to claim the rewards You have promised, and when I do, let the glory be Yours. Amen.

Keep Praying

Is anyone among you suffering? He should pray.
Is anyone cheerful? He should sing praises.

JAMES 5:13 HCSB

God is trying to get His message through *to you*. Are you listening? Hopefully so.

Perhaps, if you're experiencing tough times or uncertain times, you may find yourself overwhelmed by the press of everyday life. Perhaps you forget to slow yourself down long enough to talk with God. Instead of turning your thoughts and prayers to Him, you may rely upon our own resources. Instead of asking God for guidance, you may depend only upon your own limited wisdom. A far better course of action is this: simply stop what you're doing long enough to open your heart to God; then listen carefully for His directions.

Do you spend time each day with God? You should. Are you in need? Ask the Lord to sustain you. Are you troubled? Take your worries to Him in prayer. Are you weary? Seek God's strength. In all things great and small, seek God's wisdom and His grace. He hears your prayers, and He will answer. All you must do is ask.

Prayer pushes us through life's slumps,
propels us over the humps and pulls us out of the dumps.
Prayer is the thing we need to get the answers we seek.

MAX LUCADO

A Prayer to End Your Day

Heavenly Father, when I open my heart to You, You respond to me. Tonight, I will take my fears, my plans, and my hopes to You in prayer. Because I know that you are with me, Lord, I can end this day in peace. Amen.

Follow Him

*Then Jesus said to His disciples, "If anyone wants to come
with Me, he must deny himself, take up his cross, and follow Me.
For whoever wants to save his life will lose it,
but whoever loses his life because of Me will find it."*

MATTHEW 16:24–25 HCSB

Jesus walks with you. Are you walking with Him seven days a week, and not just on Sunday mornings? Hopefully, you understand the wisdom of walking with Christ all day every day.

Hannah Whitall Smith spoke to believers of every generation when she advised, "Keep your face upturned to Christ as the flowers do to the sun. Look, and your soul shall live and grow." That's powerful advice. When we turn our hearts to Jesus, we receive His blessings, His peace, and His grace.

Tomorrow morning, when you awaken from sleep, you will begin another day that is filled with countless opportunities to serve God and to follow in the footsteps of His Son. When you do, your heavenly Father will guide your steps and bless your endeavors. May you seek His will, may you trust His teachings, and may you walk in His footsteps—now and forever—amen.

*The crucial question for each of us is this: What do you think of Jesus,
and do you yet have a personal acquaintance with Him?*

HANNAH WHITALL SMITH

A Prayer to End Your Day

Heavenly Father, You sent Your Son so that I might have abundant life and eternal life. Thank You, Father, for my Savior, Christ Jesus. I will follow Him, honor Him, and share His Good News every day of my life. Amen.

Faith for Life

For whatever is born of God overcomes the world.
And this is the victory that has overcome the world–our faith.

1 JOHN 5:4 NKJV

The first element of a successful life is faith—faith in God, faith in His promises, and faith in His Son. If we place our lives in God's hands, our faith is rewarded in ways that we, as human beings with clouded vision and limited understanding, can scarcely comprehend. But if we seek to rely solely upon our own resources, or if we seek earthly success outside the boundaries of God's commandments, the results are predictably unfortunate.

Trust God tonight, tomorrow, and every day that you live. Then, when you have entrusted your future to the Giver of all things good, rest assured that your future is secure, not only for today, but also for eternity.

Faith is the Christian's foundation, hope is his anchor,
death is his harbor, Christ is his pilot, and heaven is his country.

JEREMY TAYLOR

A Prayer to End Your Day

Father, in the dark moments of my life, help me to remember that You are always near and that You can overcome any challenge. As I come to the end of this day, keep me mindful of Your love and Your power. And tomorrow, when I face a new day, let me live courageously and faithfully for You. Amen.

Keep Growing

But grow in the grace and knowledge of our Lord and Savior Jesus Christ. To Him be the glory both now and forever. Amen.

2 PETER 3:18 NKJV

As a Christian, you should never stop growing. No matter your age, no matter your circumstances, you have opportunities to learn and opportunities to serve. Wherever you happen to be, God is there, too, and He wants to bless you with an expanding array of spiritual gifts. Your job is to let Him.

The path to spiritual maturity unfolds day by day and moment by moment. Through prayer, through Bible study, through silence, and through humble obedience to God's Word, we can strengthen our relationship with Him. The more we focus on the Father, the more He blesses our lives. The more carefully we listen for His voice, the more He teaches us.

In the quiet moments when we open our hearts to the Lord, the Creator who made us keeps remaking us. He gives us guidance, perspective, courage, and strength. And the appropriate moment to accept these spiritual gifts is always the present one.

Spiritual maturity is becoming more and more like Christ, and if you make this your goal, it will change your life.

BILLY GRAHAM

A Prayer to End Your Day

Dear Lord, I want to grow closer to You day by day, and I know that obedience strengthens my relationship with You. Thank You, Father, for the opportunity to grow closer to You tonight, tomorrow, and every day of my life. Amen.

God Protects

When you pass through the waters, I will be with you; and through the rivers, they shall not overflow you. When you walk through the fire, you shall not be burned, nor shall the flame scorch you. For I am the LORD your God, the Holy One of Israel, your Savior.

ISAIAH 43:2-3 NKJV

As life here on earth unfolds, all of us encounter occasional disappointments and setbacks. Those occasional visits from Old Man Trouble are simply a fact of life, and none of us is exempt. When tough times arrive, we may be forced to rearrange our plans and our priorities. But even on our darkest days, we must remember that God's love remains constant.

The fact that we encounter adversity is not nearly as important as the way we choose to deal with it. When tough times arrive, we have a clear choice: we can begin the difficult work of tackling our troubles . . . or not. When we summon the courage to look Old Man Trouble squarely in the eye, he usually blinks. But if we refuse to address our problems, even the smallest annoyances have a way of growing into king-sized catastrophes.

To overcome tough times, we must build our lives on the rock that cannot be shaken; we must trust in God. And then we must get on with the hard work of tackling our problems . . . because if we don't, who will? Or should?

A Prayer to End Your Day

Dear Lord, whatever my circumstances, I will trust You. In good times and hard times, I will praise You, Father, knowing that You understand the wisdom of Your perfect plan. As I come to the end of this day, I give thanks for Your love and Your protection. I know that You are my shepherd, now and forever. Amen.

Have the Courage to Trust God

Trust in the LORD with all your heart, and do not rely on your own understanding; think about Him in all your ways, and He will guide you on the right paths.

PROVERBS 3:5-6 HCSB

Sometimes the future seems bright, and sometimes it does not. Yet even when we cannot see the possibilities of tomorrow, God can. As believers, our challenge is to trust an uncertain future to an all-powerful God.

When we trust God, we should trust Him without reservation. We should steel ourselves against the inevitable stresses of the day, secure in the knowledge that our heavenly Father has a plan for the future that only He can see.

Can you place your future into the hands of a loving and all-knowing God? Can you live amid the uncertainties of everyday life, knowing that God has dominion over all your tomorrows? If you can, you are wise and you are blessed. When you trust God with everything you are and everything you have, He will bless you now and forever.

Never be afraid to trust an unknown future to a known God.

CORRIE TEN BOOM

A Prayer to End Your Day

Dear Lord, let my faith be in You, and in You alone. Without You, I am weak, but when I trust You, I am protected. In every aspect of my life, Father, let me place my hope and my trust in Your infinite wisdom and Your boundless grace. Amen.

Guard Your Thoughts

*Finally, brothers and sisters, whatever is true,
whatever is noble, whatever is right, whatever is pure,
whatever is lovely, whatever is admirable–if anything
is excellent or praiseworthy–think about such things.*

PHILIPPIANS 4:8 NIV

English clergyman William Ralph Inge observed, "No Christian should be a pessimist, for Christianity is a system of radical optimism." Inge's words are most certainly true, but sometimes, you may find yourself pulled down by tough times. If you find yourself discouraged, exhausted, or both, then it's time to ask yourself this question: What's bothering you, and why?

If you're worried by the inevitable challenges of everyday living, God wants to help you rearrange your thoughts. After all, the ultimate battle has already been won on the cross at Calvary. And if your life has been transformed by Christ's sacrifice, then you, as a recipient of God's grace, have every reason to live courageously.

A. W. Tozer noted, "Attitude is all-important. Let the soul take a quiet attitude of faith and love toward God, and from there on, the responsibility is God's. He will make good on His commitments." These words should serve as a reminder that even when the challenges of the day seem daunting, God remains steadfast. And, so should you.

A Prayer to End Your Day

Dear Lord, tonight I will focus on Your love, Your power, Your Promises, and Your Son. When I am weak, I will turn to You for strength; when I am worried, I will turn to You for comfort; when I am troubled, I will turn to You for patience and perspective. Help me guard my thoughts, Father, so that I may honor You now and forever. Amen.

He Renews Our Strength

I will give you a new heart and put a new spirit within you.
EZEKIEL 36:26 HCSB

Even the most inspired Christians can, from time to time, find themselves running on empty. The demands of daily life can drain us of our strength and rob us of the joy that is rightfully ours in Christ. When we find ourselves tired, discouraged, or worse, there is a source from which we can draw the power needed to recharge our spiritual batteries. That source is God.

The Lord intends that His children lead joyous lives filled with abundance and peace. But sometimes, abundance and peace seem very far away. It is then that we must turn to God for renewal, and when we do, He will restore us.

Are you tired or troubled? Turn your heart toward God in prayer. Are you weak or worried? Take the time—or, more accurately, *make* the time—to delve deeply into God's Holy Word. Are you spiritually depleted? Call upon fellow believers to support you, and call upon Christ to renew your spirit and your life. When you do, you'll discover that the Creator of the universe stands always ready and always able to create a new sense of wonderment and joy in you.

God specializes in giving people a fresh start.
RICK WARREN

A Prayer to End Your Day

Lord, You are my rock and my strength. When I grow weary, let me turn my thoughts and my prayers to You. When I am discouraged, restore my faith in You. Let me always trust in Your promises, Lord, and let me draw strength from those promises and from Your unending love. Amen.

Living on Purpose

*We must do the works of Him who sent Me while it is day.
Night is coming when no one can work.*

JOHN 9:4 HCSB

God doesn't do things by accident. He didn't put you here by chance. The Lord didn't deliver you to your particular place, at this particular time, with your particular set of talents and opportunities on a whim. He has a plan, a one-of-a-kind mission designed especially for you. Discovering that plan may take time. But if you keep asking God for guidance, He'll lead you along a path of His choosing and give you every tool you need to fulfill His will.

Of course, you'll probably encounter a few impediments as you attempt to discover the exact nature of God's purpose for your life. And you may travel down a few dead ends along the way. But if you keep searching, and if you genuinely seek the Lord's guidance, He'll reveal His plans at a time and place of His own choosing.

Tonight, tomorrow, and every day of your life, God is beckoning you to hear His voice. When you listen—and when you answer His call—you'll be amazed at the wonderful things that an all-knowing, all-powerful God can do.

If you're alive, there's a purpose for your life.

RICK WARREN

A Prayer to End Your Day

Heavenly Father, I know that You have a plan for my life, and I will continue to seek that plan. Give me the wisdom to understand Your purpose for me, dear Lord, and give me courage to serve You with my thoughts, with my prayers, and with my life. Amen.

The Wisdom to be Hopeful

Now if any of you lacks wisdom, he should ask God, who gives to all generously and without criticizing, and it will be given to him. But let him ask in faith without doubting. For the doubter is like the surging sea, driven and tossed by the wind.

JAMES 1:5-6 HCSB

Wisdom and hope are traveling companions. Wise men and women learn to think optimistically about their lives, their futures, and their faith. The pessimists, however, are not so fortunate; they choose instead to focus their thoughts and energies on faultfinding, criticizing, and complaining, with precious little to show for their efforts.

To become wise, we must seek God's wisdom—the wisdom of hope—and we must live according to God's Word. To become wise, we must seek God's guidance with consistency and purpose. To become wise, we must not only learn the lessons of life, we must live by them.

Do you seek wisdom for yourself and for your family? Then remember this: the ultimate source of wisdom is the Word of God. When you study God's Word and live in accordance with His teachings, you will grow wise, you will remain hopeful, and you will be a blessing to your family and to the world.

A Prayer to End Your Day

Dear Lord, when I depend upon the world's wisdom, I make many mistakes. But when I trust Your wisdom, I build my life on a firm foundation. Tonight, tomorrow, and every day of my life, I will trust Your Word and follow it, knowing that the ultimate wisdom is Your wisdom and the ultimate truth is Your truth. Amen.

He Is Your Strength and Protector

When a suffering woman sought healing by simply touching the hem of His garment, Jesus turned and said, "Daughter, be of good comfort; thy faith hath made thee whole" (Matthew 9:22 KJV). We, too, can be made whole when we place our faith, completely and without reservation, in the person of Jesus Christ.

Concentration camp survivor Corrie ten Boom relied on faith during her ten months of imprisonment and torture. Later, despite the fact that four of her family members had died in Nazi death camps, Corrie's faith was unshaken. She wrote, "There is no pit so deep that God's love is not deeper still." Christians take note: genuine faith in God means faith in all circumstances, happy or sad, joyful or tragic.

If you reach out to Him in faith, He will give you peace and heal your broken spirit. Be content to touch even the smallest fragment of the Master's garment, and He will make you whole.

A Prayer to End Your Day

Dear Lord, You are my strength and my protector. I will turn to You, Lord, when I am weak. In times of adversity, I will trust Your plan, and whatever my circumstances, Father, I will look to You for strength, wisdom, and courage. Amen.

Actions Speak Louder

The old saying is both familiar and true: actions indeed speak louder than words. As believers, we must beware: our actions should always give credence to the changes that Christ can make in the lives of those who walk with Him.

If we are to be responsible believers, we must realize that it is never enough simply to hear the instructions of God; we must also live by them. Doing God's work is a responsibility that each of us must bear, and when we do, our loving heavenly Father rewards our efforts with a bountiful harvest.

So if you if you'd like to renew your strength or jumpstart your life, ask God to give you the strength and the wisdom to do first things first, even if the first thing is hard. And while you're at it, employ less talk and more action. Because a thousand good intentions pale in comparison to a single good deed.

A Prayer to End Your Day

Dear Lord, as I come to the end of this day, I am mindful of Your presence and Your love. Tonight, I pray for guidance. And I pray that by following in the footsteps of Your Son, others might see Him through me. Amen.

93

Keep Studying His Word

A. W. Tozer wrote, "The purpose of the Bible is to bring men to Christ, to make them holy and prepare them for heaven. In this it is unique among books, and it always fulfills its purpose." And George Mueller observed, "The vigor of our spiritual lives will be in exact proportion to the place held by the Bible in our lives and in our thoughts." As Christians, we are called upon to study God's Holy Word and then to share it with the world.

The Bible is a priceless gift, a tool for Christians to use as they share the Good News of their Savior, Christ Jesus. Too many Christians, however, keep their spiritual tool kits tightly closed and out of sight.

God's Holy Word is a priceless, one-of-a-kind treasure. Handle it with care, but more importantly, handle it every day.

A Prayer to End Your Day

Dear Lord, the Bible is Your gift to me. When I place Your Word at the very center of my life, I am blessed. So tonight I ask that You help me focus on Your Word so that I might be a faithful servant in Your world. Amen.

Be Patient and Trust God

Be still before the LORD and wait patiently for Him.
PSALM 37:7 NIV

Psalm 37:7 commands us to wait patiently for God. But as busy people in a fast-paced world, many of us find that waiting quietly for God is difficult. Why? Because we are fallible human beings seeking to live according to our own timetables, not God's. In our better moments, we realize that patience is not only a virtue, but it is also a commandment from God.

We human beings are impatient by nature. We know what we want, and we know exactly when we want it: right now. But God knows better. He has created a world that unfolds according to His plans, not our own. As thoughtful Christians, we must trust His wisdom and His goodness.

God instructs us to be patient in *all* things. We must be patient with our families, our friends, and our associates. We must also be patient with our Creator as He unfolds His plan for our lives. And that's as it should be. After all, think how patient God has been *with us*.

God never hurries. There are no deadlines against which He must work. To know this is to quiet our spirits and relax our nerves.
A. W. TOZER

A Prayer to End Your Day

Lord, give me patience. When I am hurried, give me peace. When I am frustrated, give me perspective. When I am angry, let me turn my heart to You. Tonight, I will trust Your timetable, Lord, and I will trust Your master plan for my life. Amen.

Be Optimistic

My cup runs over. Surely goodness and mercy shall follow me all the days of my life; and I will dwell in the house of the LORD forever.

PSALM 23:5–6 NKJV

Are you an optimistic, hopeful, enthusiastic Christian? You should be. After all, as a believer, you have every reason to be optimistic about life here on earth and life eternal. As C. H. Spurgeon observed, "Our hope in Christ for the future is the mainstream of our joy." But sometimes you may find yourself pulled down by the inevitable demands and worries of life here on earth. If you find yourself discouraged, stressed, or both, then it's time to take your concerns to God. When you do, He will lift your spirits and renew your strength.

Tonight, make this promise to yourself and keep it: vow to be a hope-filled Christian. Think optimistically about your life, your family, and your future. Trust your hopes, not your fears. And then, when you've filled your heart with hope and gladness, offer a prayer of thanks to your Creator for a life — your life — that that will be richly blessed tonight, tomorrow, and throughout eternity.

Two types of voices command your attention today. Negative ones fill your mind with doubt, bitterness, and fear. Positive ones purvey hope and strength. Which one will you choose to heed?

MAX LUCADO

A Prayer to End Your Day

Dear Lord, I will look for the best in other people; I will expect the best from You; and I will try my best to do my best with joy in my heart and praise on my lips. Amen.

Facing Those Fears

Don't be afraid, for I am with you. Don't be discouraged,
for I am your God. I will strengthen you and help you.
I will hold you up with my victorious right hand.
ISAIAH 41:10 NLT

We live in a world that is, at times, a frightening place. We live in a world that is, at times, a discouraging place. We live in a world where life-changing losses can be so painful and so profound that it seems we may never recover. But with God's help, and with the help of encouraging family members and friends, we can recover.

During the darker days of life, we are wise to remember the words of Jesus, who reassured His disciples, saying, "Take courage! It is I. Don't be afraid" (Matthew 14:27 NIV). Then, when we've been reassured by the words of Jesus, we can offer encouragement to others. And by helping them face *their* fears, we can, in turn, tackle *our own* problems with courage, with determination, and with faith.

So the next time you're attacked by irrational fears, don't let them hijack your thoughts and don't let them rule your life. Instead, have courage. Your Shepherd is with you, and you're protected.

Meet your fears with faith.
MAX LUCADO

A Prayer to End Your Day

Heavenly Father, even when I walk through the valley of the shadow of death, I will fear no evil because You are with me. Thank You, Lord, for Your perfect love, a love that casts out fear and gives me the strength and the courage to meet any challenge. Amen.

Forgive Everybody

*Be kind to one another, tender-hearted, forgiving each other,
just as God in Christ also has forgiven you.*

EPHESIANS 4:32 NASB

Forgiveness, no matter how difficult, is God's way, and it must be our way too. Sometimes, of course, forgiveness is difficult. Being frail, fallible, imperfect human beings, we are quick to anger, quick to blame, slow to forgive, and even slower to forget. But we should not use these human frailties as an excuse to disobey God.

God's commandments are not intended to be customized for the particular whims of particular believers. God's word is not a menu from which each of us may select items à la carte, according to our own desires. Far from it. God's Holy Word is a book that must be taken in its entirety; all of God's commandments are to be taken seriously. And so it is with forgiveness.

So tonight, as a gift to yourself and to your loved ones, forgive everyone who has ever harmed you. Then claim the inner peace that is your spiritual birthright: the peace of Jesus Christ. It is always available; it has been paid for in full; it is yours for the asking. So ask, receive, and share.

*Forgiveness is one of the most beautiful words
in the human vocabulary. How much pain could be avoided
if we all learned the meaning of this word!*

BILLY GRAHAM

A Prayer to End Your Day

Heavenly Father, genuine forgiveness is difficult. Help me to forgive those who have injured me, and deliver me from the traps of anger and bitterness. Forgiveness is Your way, Lord; let it be my way too. Amen.

He Offers Peace

Peace I leave with you; My peace I give to you; not as the world gives do I give to you. Do not let your heart be troubled, nor let it be fearful.

JOHN 14:27 NASB

These are turbulent times when worries are easy to identify and peace seems to be a scarce commodity. But no times are too turbulent for God. And if you sincerely desire the peace that passes all understanding, you'll find it in Him.

The familiar words of John 14:27 remind us that Jesus offers us peace, not as the world gives, but as He alone gives. Have you found the genuine peace that can be yours through Jesus Christ? Or are you still rushing after the illusion of "peace and happiness" that the world promises but cannot deliver?

When you welcome God's love into your heart, your life will be transformed as the Father's peace will become yours. And then, because you possess the gift of peace, you can share that gift with family members, with friends, and with coworkers.

So thank your heavenly Father, study His Word, and follow as closely as you can in the footsteps of His Son. It's the right thing to do—in good times and in hard times—and it's the peaceful way to live.

Peace does not dwell in outward things, but in the heart prepared to wait trustfully and quietly on Him who has all things safely in His hands.

ELISABETH ELLIOT

A Prayer to End Your Day

Dear Lord, tonight I open my heart to You. And I thank You, God, for Your love, for Your peace, and for Your Son. Amen.

Instead of Worrying, Trust

Blessed is the one who trusts in the LORD.
PROVERBS 16:20 NIV

Because you have the ability to think, you also have the ability to worry. Even if you're a very faithful Christian, you may be plagued by occasional periods of discouragement and doubt. Even though you trust God's promise of salvation—even though you sincerely believe in God's love and protection—you may find yourself upset by the inevitable frustrations of everyday life.

Where is the best place to take your worries? Take them to God. Take your troubles to Him; take your fears to Him; take your doubts to Him; take your weaknesses to Him; take your frustrations to Him, and leave them all there. Seek protection from the One who offers you eternal salvation; build your spiritual house upon the Rock that cannot be moved. Then you can spend your time and energy solving the problems you can fix while trusting God to do the rest.

It has been well said that no man ever sank under the burden of the day. It is when tomorrow's burden is added to the burden of today that the weight is more than a man can bear. Never load yourselves so, my friends. If you find yourselves so loaded, at least remember this: it is your own doing, not God's. He begs you to leave the future to Him and mind the present.
GEORGE MACDONALD

A Prayer to End Your Day

Dear Lord, when I am tempted to lose faith in the future, give me courage. When I am fearful, keep me mindful that You are my shepherd. Give me strength, Father, to face the challenges of everyday life, and give me the wisdom to seek comfort and courage from You. Amen.

Why God Sent His Son

For God so loved the world that He gave His only begotten Son, that whoever believes in Him should not perish but have everlasting life.
JOHN 3:16 NKJV

God's love for you is deeper and more profound than you can imagine. God's love for you is so great that He sent His only Son to this earth to die for your sins and to offer you the priceless gift of eternal life. Now you must decide whether or not to accept God's gift. Will you ignore it or embrace it? Will you return it or neglect it? Will you accept Christ, or will you turn from Him?

Your decision to accept Christ is the pivotal decision of your life. It is a decision that you cannot ignore. It is a decision that is yours and yours alone. It is a decision with eternal consequences. Accept God's gift: Accept Christ now.

Jesus became mortal to give you immortality;
and today, through Him, you can be free.
DAVID JEREMIAH

A Prayer to End Your Day

Dear Lord, You sent Your Son to this earth that we might have the gift of eternal life. Tonight I thank You, Father, for that priceless gift. Give me the strength to share the wondrous message of Jesus with others so that they, too, might accept Him as their Savior. Amen.